Henry Alford

Meditations in advent, on creation, and on providence

Henry Alford

Meditations in advent, on creation, and on providence

ISBN/EAN: 9783742845061

Manufactured in Europe, USA, Canada, Australia, Japa

Cover: Foto ©Andreas Hilbeck / pixelio.de

Manufactured and distributed by brebook publishing software (www.brebook.com)

Henry Alford

Meditations in advent, on creation, and on providence

MEDITATIONS

IN ADVENT, ON CREATION, AND
ON PROVIDENCE

By HENRY ALFORD, D.D.
DEAN OF CANTERBURY

ALEXANDER STRAHAN, PUBLISHER
148 STRAND, LONDON
1865

PREFACE.

THESE Meditations, which were originally preached as Sermons in Canterbury Cathedral, all follow one course and form of thought. I have taken some of the great familiar truths of our religious belief or life, and, stripping them of accidents and conventionalities, have endeavoured to lay them forth in their reality, face to face with our ordinary thoughts and habits. The first result of this procedure naturally has been, that the two appear incompatible with each other. Truth has been so much wrapped up in the conventional terms of theology, that when disengaged from them, its most familiar examples assume a strange aspect, and break in abruptly on the tenor of our thoughts.

Then, working from this point, I have tried to shew that the contrast is in fact apparent only: that matters of the same kind as these great truths are recognised in our ordinary lives: and that a fair and candid mind is no more justified in refusing credence to these articles of our faith, than it is in ignoring the every-day phenomena of man's existence.

In tracing out these analogies, I have been occasionally led to touch on some common ways of speaking and thinking, which usually meet with severe reprobation, and to maintain that such reprobation is undeserved. In this case also, the facts of human nature have been obscured by our craving after systematic precision. While the teachers of theology have been careful to draw their lines of demarcation sharply, and to satisfy the expectations of public religious opinion, the great currents of human instinct and desire have been flowing

PREFACE.

on, irrespective of their teaching, and for the most part, unrecognised by them. Yet it is by their instincts and desires that our persuasion must lay hold of the hearts of our hearers. And it is to these that our Blessed Lord in His discourses, and His Apostles in their writings, constantly make appeal.

It seems plain that, in order to render our pulpit ministrations effective, we must condescend to make use, far more than we do, of men's ordinary thoughts and words: and to enter into and deal with, not imaginary states of mind and affection, not imaginary difficulties, but those really felt by our hearers.

BOCHASTLE, CALLANDER,
September, 1865.

CONTENTS.

IN ADVENT.

	PAGE
I. THE LORD'S COMING	1
II. THE GREAT ACCOUNT	18
III. PRACTICAL EFFECT ON LIFE	37
IV. NO CHANGE IN NATURE	50

ON CREATION 71

ON PROVIDENCE.

I. DIFFICULTIES OF THE MAIN SUBJECT	131
II. GOD'S GUIDANCE OF US FOR GOOD	150
III. TESTIMONY FROM THE COURSE OF THE WORLD	167
IV. DIVINE AND HUMAN AGENCY	186
V. EFFECT ON MEN OF GOD'S ORDINARY AND EXTRAORDINARY DEALINGS	204
VI. GOD'S ESTIMATE OF HIS OWN WORKS	223

IN ADVENT.

I.

THE LORD'S COMING.

It seems very difficult to conceive that the usual course of this world should ever be broken in upon by such an event as the coming of our Lord. It forms one of the most startling contrasts possible, to place side by side the common every-day thoughts of all of us about things around us, and the reality of the appearance of our Lord Jesus Christ in the midst of us. Of what is this a sign? On the one hand, do not let us press it further than is fair. I suppose something of the kind is the case with us about all very solemn things. We all know we must die; but a sentence of death, or the discovery of that fatal necessity imminent on us, would be to any of us a rude shock to our ordinary habits and thoughts. We all believe the holy articles of our faith; but there are times in the lives of us all, times of which we have no reason to be ashamed, when the mention of these solemn points of our belief would come in strangely and incongruously. So that I think we must not hold the fact with which we set out to be in itself a sign of irreligion. It is rather, perhaps, a necessity of our nature. God has so made us, that we are necessarily taken hold of and possessed by the things about us. The things that are not seen are of infinitely more importance: but it is the things that are seen' which are present and nearest us. We must make an effort to look at the one; the other we cannot help seeing. And so it is, that while God has constituted us beneficently in this respect, so that this tendency of our nature is good for us in the main—good for our preservation in life, good for our enjoyment of life, good for our success in life—yet, like all our other natural tendencies and habits, it needs correcting, needs elevating, needs to be interfered with, for the purposes of our best and highest life. For we are not, while in this present state, to be the slaves of outward things; and by far the greater part of our existence will be passed in another state than this, even an eternal one.

Thoughts like these, naturally arising out of the great subject of Advent, seem to lead us to shape our meditations thus:—The *difficulty* of realizing our Lord's coming, as necessarily belonging to our ordinary life in this world; and the *necessity* of realizing the Lord's coming, as belonging to the better part of our life here, and to our higher life hereafter. May God guide and bless us while we think on these two things.

" Yet a little while, and He that shall come will come." This is our belief. But *when?* and *how?* How many centuries have sped by since these words were written! How many more may drag on before they are fulfilled! Where in our own days, where in days future, can we assign a time when we can realize the fact of His coming? Shall it be while earth is at peace, amidst the steady labours of the arts, and while man's thoughts are even and undistracted? Shall the merchant on the exchange, the student at his desk, the traveller on his journey, the mother in her family duties, the children in their school or at their play, be startled with the cry of His approach? So seem some places in Holy Scripture to teach us; and yet how difficult to imagine it! What do any of us expect less, than such a surprise in such employments? What seems more unlike God's ways of dealing with man during all these centuries, than that such a sudden crash should break in upon this settled order of things, which He has so far established, that it is our duty to Him to see it maintained, and to keep its place among ourselves? Well, but let us then take the other alternative. Shall that day come upon us amidst fierce wars and distresses, when men's passions are let loose, and their thoughts have lost balance? Shall the ears of the wild combatants in the battle-field be pierced by the shout of the archangel rising over the din of their conflict? Shall the lurid glare of burning homes usher in the conflagration of the heaven and the earth? Shall anguish and mourning be already upon mankind, before that sign shall appear in heaven at which all the tribes of the earth shall mourn? This again seems not inconsistent with the testimony of Scripture in other places. But in that case how difficult to imagine God's faithful people waiting and praying; how must their thoughts be distracted, and their Saviour put out of their sight, by the dire necessities of the time! If the Christian prays against sudden death, if he dreads the passing from perhaps a light jest, or a trifling thought, or a festal moment, to the presence of his God, who would expect that the Church shall then, so to speak, be taken at a disadvantage, when fierce passions are raging even in bosoms whose law is forgiveness, and the ordinary means of grace are suspended? Again, if we put the alternative as to different times of our ordinary life, we shall find it equally difficult to give reality to our expectations of the Lord's coming. Hear what the poet sings of it:—

> "At midnight, when mankind is wrapt in peace,
> And worldly fancy feeds on golden dreams:
> To give more dread to man's most dreadful hour,
> At midnight, 'tis presumed, this pomp will burst
> From tenfold darkness: sudden as the spark
> From smitten steel: from nitrous grain the blaze.
> Man, starting from his couch, shall sleep no more!
> The day is broke, which never more shall close!" *

* Young, "Night Thoughts."

Now as to this,—we know that "that day will come as a thief in the night;" and to some it must, like the thief, come in the night itself. But it is impossible to apply this to all mankind, seeing that night and day share our globe alike, and such a consideration entirely prevents any general application of such a description, or of any description of men's occupations, except on the largest scale, when it shall overtake them. They shall be "eating and drinking, marrying and giving in marriage, buying and selling, planting and building;" these shall be their general employments over the whole earth: on such things shall their thoughts be; but to give any detailed description of the circumstance as applicable to all men is, from the above reason, impossible. Then, again, as to the *place* where the Lord shall come, how difficult it is to form any idea in our minds which may at all accord with the facts and laws of nature to which we find ourselves subjected! He shall come and be seen by all; by all at the same moment; so that the very conditions of our senses will be changed, the very foundations of the earth broken up, all present hindrances removed. All the channels of thought and perception must be different, before such a thing can be. And here we seem to have arrived at the true reason of the difficulty which we find in conceiving this matter,—that it does not belong to our present state or perceptions; we shall be changed before we are conscious of it; in that change, all incongruity will pass away; after it, all surprise will have vanished in its surpassing greatness. Our eyes will see the Lord: but not these eyes, whose vision is limited by so brief a space; not these, which find obstacles in matter intervening; not these, which weep earthly tears, and glance aside at earthly vanities. Our ears will hear the voice before which heaven and earth shall flee away; but not these earthly organs, ever hearing amiss, unable to distinguish the good from the vain. Our hearts shall beat high at the joy of our Lord's approach; yet not these feeble ones, the strongest of which would be arrested in its vital course by terror at the very adjuncts of his coming; but other and more blessed ones, even new hearts, able to welcome all his glory, and to respond to all his love. We shall be changed—through the grave or without the grave—all changed, so that earth will be different to us, time will be different, other men will be different, ourselves will be different; for He that sitteth on the Throne will have made all things new.

The difficulty, then, in conceiving the coming of the Lord, is incident to our present state, belongs to the imperfection of our present faculties, and to their necessary connection with the things of sense and of this world. We shall never lose it. As long as we are in this state, it will be a strange thing to us that the Lord should come and put an end to this state, and break up all the habits and associations of the world which lies about us.

Now this difficulty affects the unbeliever in one way, and the Christian in another. It confirms the unbeliever in his unbelief. "Where is the promise of His coming? for all things remain as they were from the beginning of the creation." This is the language of the unbeliever; in the days of St. Peter, and in our days. The stability of Nature and her laws, the difficulty of conceiving the Lord's coming in upon and interrupting the present order of things, is to him a reason for disbelieving altogether that He will come—for setting at nought the hopes of the Christian Church, and expecting that this world is to last for ever as it is.

On the Christian believer the effect is very different. He, if he be wise, does not pretend in this matter to be differently situated from other men. Their difficulties are his difficulties. He can no more realize the dread and sudden event than they can. Where it is to be, how it is to be, these are mysteries to him as to others. But what is his conclusion from these difficulties and mysteries? Is it this, that he should relax his hold on belief in the great fact itself; that he should let go his faith in Him who hath promised, and cease to look and wait for the coming of the Lord? Nay, if I know anything of the ordinary course of the working of the Christian's thoughts, it is the direct reverse of this. The certainty of the event itself is beyond doubt. All Scripture is pledged to it; our Lord's own most sacred word is pledged to it again and again. If the assurance, "He that shall come will come," had never been written, it would yet have been virtually written over and over again that He will come, and will not tarry. Here there can be no giving way. This at least is an article of his faith: and without believing this, he could not be the Christian which he is. What then is his inference from this difficulty on which we have been treating?—from the fact, that is, that this solemn coming of his Lord is a matter not belonging to the state of time, not easily occurring to, nor grasped by, our present senses and faculties? What can it be but this,—that it needs so much the more to be thought upon, to be made matter of earnest meditation, to be surveyed in all its great bearings on his thoughts and desires, on his affections and determinations? "Seeing these things are so, what manner of men," as St. Peter asks, " ought we to be?" Seeing it is certain that this present state of things will come to a sudden end by the Advent of our Lord, how ought we to think of men and things around us; how to make our plans; how truly to enjoy life; how to deny ourselves; how to feel God's presence about and over us; how to war against sin and evil; how to perform the various duties of our stations for which we shall on that day be called to account? For this is another result of that of which we have been speaking: that our preparation for that day must rather consist in the things that are, than in those which are to be. Its events are great, and beyond our comprehension: strange, and removed out of our experience. If we were always to be dwelling on them, ever speculating on them, we should be forsaking our line of practical good, and unfitting ourselves for God's work, which lies in every man's path of life. Nay, the attempt would be vain; vain, as we saw, for any worthy comprehension which it would give us of that day; vain for any imagined success in throwing off the realities of this state in which we are. For the *present*, which lies about a man, wraps him like a garment, and gives the form and semblance to all his thoughts and deeds; the age in which a man lives is the very flesh and blood of his personal being, and he can no more divest himself of it and be separate from it, than he can divest himself of those and be separate from them.

In our daily work then it is, that we must prepare for Christ's coming: in the occupations of this day, for the account of that day: by living more purely, more truthfully, more charitably: living more in prayer, more in consciousness of God's presence, more in the cleansing power of the Lord's blessed Atonement, and by the guidance of His indwelling Spirit.

One thought may perhaps have been in some minds, as they have been reading these lines: and it is this, Will not the Lord's coming, to most of us, in all probability be the day of our own death? And would it not be more profitable to be preparing us for that, than to write to us of an event which may be far distant, and probably will not come on the earth in our time at all? To this question there are two answers, —answers which ought to be ever impressed on a Christian's mind. First, the view of things proposed by the inquirer is not that taken in Holy Scripture, which is the rule and pattern of our teaching. There we do not hear anything of preparation for *death*. I doubt whether one text can be found in which we are exhorted to make such preparation, *as such*. But the constant note, the continually recurring exhortation is, to be prepared for the Lord's coming. So that if we would teach as God's word teaches, as our blessed Lord and his Apostles taught, we cannot do as the inquirer would have us. Our second answer goes to the reason of the thing, and in fact gives the account and lays open the foundation of the former. He who is prepared for the Lord's coming, is necessarily also prepared for his own death. The greater includes the less. He who so lives, so thinks, so speaks, so works, in his daily life, as to be ready for the sign of the Son of man in heaven, and the voice of the archangel, and the trump of God, will not be found unready when the summons is heard in a softer tone, and comes with more previous warning. If he can meet the Lord amidst the flaming heavens and the gathering dead, he will not be loath to obey His call, when its dread reality is tempered with all gentle and kindly alleviation—with the gradual approaches of sickness and infirmity, and the tender solaces of loving friends and watchful attendants. But, on the other hand, he who has forgotten his Lord's coming, and has simply been careful about readiness for his own dismissal, will ever be too liable in the lesser thing to have neglected care for the greater; and he will also be well-nigh certain to have lowered his standard of attainment, and narrowed his sympathies, unworthily; in taking thought for himself, to have forgotten the great Body of which he is a member; in minding his own safety, to have forgotten the glory of his Lord—nay, his very Lord Himself.

For—and with this thought we will draw to a close—there is nothing that so much takes a man out of himself; nothing that so much raises and widens his thoughts and sympathies; nothing that so much purifies and elevates his hopes, as this preparation for the coming of the Lord.

One thought more. And it is on words occurring in a text already more than once referred to, "Yet a little while." I said it was not good to speculate, not good to give scope to the roving fancy, as to the great event, its manner or its time. Still these words, "Yet a little while," should be impressed on every mind. Could we look at the future as we do on the past,—could we estimate the interval of time between the Lord's first and second coming, as we shall do when we look back on it from the eternal state,—how short it would seem! And how short it really is to Him who inhabiteth eternity! "Yet a little while:"—long perhaps to us, distracted with our petty interests, harassed with our unresting cares, biassed by our cherished prejudices; but in itself, and in our real lifetime, short indeed. And if but a little while, how much the more important! How full should it be of life's work, life's seedtime, life's decision!

Oh let us live it for God and for good; let us live it for the day which shall end it; let us live it as we shall wish we had done when we see the Son of man on his Throne, come to judge the world!

II.

THE GREAT ACCOUNT.

ANOTHER train of thought which suggests itself to us in the season of Advent is this:—It is the plain and general testimony of Holy Scripture, that at the last awful day every one of us shall be judged for, and called upon to give an account of, the deeds, words, and thoughts of this present state of time: "We must all be made manifest before the judgment-seat of Christ: that every one may receive the things done in his body, whether (it be) good or bad" (2 Cor. v. 10). And even so spoke the

Preacher in the Old Testament: "God shall bring every work into judgment, with every secret thing, whether it be good or whether it be evil" (Eccles. xii. 14). And, like the persuasion of that day itself being certain to come, so likewise is this belief accepted by every Christian.

Let us examine this in dependence on God's help. Let us see what difficulties lie about the true understanding of this, as we did with the other, and endeavour to deduce here also the true estimate and idea which we ought to form of that great final account, and the right and best way of preparing for it.

Now, if we minutely inquire what it is that we really believe, when we say that we shall give account before God of all the deeds, words, and thoughts of this state, we shall find that it is one of the most astonishing things imaginable. One may be very familiar with the words; and that which they express to us may have become a well-known and accustomed thing; but depend on it, there never was anything more difficult to imagine, or to give any conceivable account of. All the deeds, words, and thoughts of our life on earth,—why, where are they? Where are those of any assignable portion of that life? If the Judge is to carry conviction to the hearts of those who shall then be judged, they surely must be in possession, at the time, of the full consciousness of each act as having been performed by them, of each word as having been spoken, of each thought as having passed through their minds. Take but one example. Suppose the great Judge to arraign me in the matter of one day of my childhood, and I were charged thus: That at such a time in it I disobeyed my parents; at such another time I showed envy, or malice, or selfishness towards my fellows; at such another time I had high thoughts of myself, or rebellious thoughts against God; and suppose all this were to be to me only as a tale that is told, only as something said about another person, and not about myself: I might not, indeed I could not, doubt the assurance, nor deny the arraignment of an infallible Judge; but where, I ask, would be the conviction in my own breast that the Judge of all the earth had done right? Unless I could see and feel at that dread moment all the sinfulness of my then acts; in other words, unless I could put myself into the very circumstances which then surrounded me, how could I give account of, how could I render in myself a true verdict concerning those long past offences? I say, the very circumstances which then surrounded me. For the guilt of my disobedience on that alleged occasion would not appear in its true light, unless I saw and knew how that dear parent was striving to win me by kindness, how prayers were rising for me, and tears were shed over me, by one whose tender heart I was of set purpose wounding; my envy, and malice, and selfishness would not be to me what it really was, unless I could see those companions of my childhood again, and recall their fresh young faces, and the tone of voices long, long forgotten; and the exceeding sinfulness of my rebel risings against my God would not come up before me, unless I could again have in me that rich and full tide of exuberant blessedness with which the God of love endows our happy childhood, and which none of us has known since he was a child. And I have taken but one instance—one day or hour long passed away. Think then how infinitely this difficulty must be multiplied, when we have to deal with not a day nor an hour, nor one frame of mind, nor one set of sins, but every hour of all days of this whole life.

And then, again, take the difficulty in this other light. What do we really know about those deeds, words, thoughts, that we can remember and recall? What, I mean, do we know of them in all their bearings, with all their extenuations, all their aggravations, all their consequences for good or for ill? At such a time we spoke an unkind word, we depreciated a good act, we were wanting in reverence for holy things. And our word or our act was like a stone thrown on the pool, and a circle of unhappy influences spread out from it, and then another and then another, even till those were the worse for it who perhaps never heard of it or of us, until time and oblivion smoothed the ripples and effaced the remembrance. But all this who can recall? Who, indeed, even knows? And yet of all this, of every item of it, shall we have to give an account. As I sit and meditate on this, I find it one of the most difficult things possible to shape in any way before my imagination. Yet shape it somehow I must, if I would meditate on it profitably.

I see, then, by what we have already taken into account, that two necessities seem to have presented themselves, in order for that day's account to be a just and a complete account. To these we shall have, I believe, by-and-by to add a third. But first let us look these fairly in the face, and thus approach that third; and when we have done this, let us inquire whether there is, as far as we can see, any reasonable prospect of these necessary things being done for us, in order to that day's account.

Well then, our first necessity, in order that we may recognize at all the deeds, words, and thoughts then laid to our charge, is this, that we be at that day cognizant of them as our own. And let there be no mistake as to what this amounts to. It amounts to nothing less than the complete restoration to us of the remembrance of the whole of our lives day by day, and hour by hour. Nothing short of this will answer the purpose. What I just now said of one day's sins, and one day's events, must be done with regard to every day's sins and every day's events. All our past life must be spread out before us, delineated with far more accuracy than the most perfect map delineates to the traveller the country he has passed through. The delineation must be (for we need not shrink from applying the wonders of science and art to illustrate such a matter) less like a map drawn by common hands, than like a photograph of the way passed over—in which inspection may detect even the minutest plant by the wayside, and the microscope may even find the nest lodged in the cleft of the rock. It must be as complete as this; for if the minutest portion of that which compounded an action, that which prompted a word, that which constituted a thought, be beyond our reach on that day, so far the Great Judge will not be in our minds and consciences justified when He shall speak, and clear when He shall judge. And we may well say, What a marvellous condition of our future judgment this is! How improbable! most would think; nay, some might even pronounce it impossible. That we should ever stand and look back over life, as a man would look on the wonderful sun-picture just now described; that we should be able to make each day and hour give up its acts and thoughts, which now seem to us as much perished and scattered as the elements of a decayed body which have passed into other bodies,—is not this a wonder passing wonder? Yet I seem to see that, if I have to give up a satisfactory final account of all my thoughts, words, and acts, I must be furnished with this and nothing short of this. But I must have more, very much more, as our former thoughts led us to see. I must have not only the restored memory of all I ever have known, but I must have the knowledge imparted to me of very much that I never have known at all. I shall want not only the forgotten dream restored, but also the interpretation of the dream furnished. Remember what was said about the unknown and untraced consequences of that which we think and do and say. Of all these undoubtedly is our responsibility made up, and by them will our account be swelled. And unless all this is present to me, as well as to my Great Judge, in that day, how is the full justice of my sentence to be comprehended by me? or, to put the blessed alternative suggested by the bright hopes of every Christian, how is the full measure of that wondrous grace of the Son of God to be seen by me, how that mighty mercy glorified which has buried my sins in its depths, and magnified itself in my utter unworthiness? So that this is our second necessity, in order for that final account to be what we believe it will be; not only must all memory be restored, but knowledge must be given far surpassing that which the keenest-sighted of men in this state ever attained to; knowledge of facts to which we never had access, of men's thoughts and words and deeds, and the complications of their private resolves, and their social intercourse, and actings upon themselves and upon one another. And if we ask, To what does this point? what is the least requirement that will satisfy this condition? I answer, and any thinking man might answer, Nothing less than the complete restoration of all that has been done in the state of time; the restoration not merely of each individual man's memory as to all that happened to himself, but of the universal memory of mankind as to all that ever happened to this world. Here, the history of the world is written by men in books; but what is written, even when we have set aside human fallibility, and the amount of the writer's own individual bias and misrepresentation, is but a very small portion of that which has really been done—only the barest outline, so to speak, with a figure here and there, of a picture which should have been absolutely filled in with life, and crowded with action. There, God will have written the history of His own world; written it without a defect or omission, without a flaw or misrepresentation; and written it for all to read. If this be not so, how can those grander responsibilities ever be understood, which we all solemnly believe to exist? How shall the great moral account of nations and of churches ever be given in the sight and hearing of the universe, unless the bearings of human policy, and the consequences of human delinquencies, on a larger scale than any individual account could take in, be open for all to see?

There seem then to be two requisites for the reality and the justice of our great final account; the full restoration of memory, and the opening of the book of knowledge, so that there has been nothing hid that shall not be known.

But now comes up before us the third condition, which I just now anticipated. Suppose both those others to be fulfilled; all memory restored, all knowledge of fact laid open; yet more even than these would be wanted. If I had them both, and yet were no fairer judge in my own case than I am now, I could not recognize in myself the justice of the Judge, nor could I glorify Him, as I humbly believe I shall do, for His mercy. We have, in this present state, no clear views of justice at all. The rights and wrongs of men are measured by a standard altogether inadequate to their apportionment. And if this is so in the case of other men abstractedly, much more is it so in the case of ourselves, much more is it so in the case of other men, when they come into contact with ourselves. Probably no man yet ever passed a right judgment on an act of his own. Give way to ordinary vanity, and we are disposed to defend all our acts, and make them seem better; check ordinary vanity, and in the very pride of conscious self-abasement, we lash ourselves too severely, and vilify the past that we may congratulate ourselves on the present.

All this will need setting right, in order for that final account to be a true and a just one. We must see things as God sees them, before God's judgment of them will cause us to lay our hand on our mouth and own Him to be right. We must look upon ourselves divested of selfishness, upon others without all that antagonism which we feel to them as obstacles to our self-esteem, in order to know and feel fully, that both we and they have our true meed at the hands of the Great Dispenser of all men's doom. If, as we know, in that day the first shall be last, and the last first, it is only thus that the first can subside into the last without bitter disappointment: only thus that they can see the last pass by them without envy and murmuring: only thus that the last can go up higher without losing their humility.

It seems then, that the restoration to all men of a perfectly righteous standard of judging both themselves and others is another necessary condition, in order that that final account may be a reality for us, and produce its solemn effects; for bliss, and, we might have said, for woe also.

And now let us see whether we possess, in the present state of things, any however faint indications that these conditions are possible or probable for us.

First, as to the entire restoration of the individual memory. What is it to forget? What, but to have lost our mental grasp on something which once we held within it? If this grasp have been but recently lost, the fact escaped may generally be found with but little trouble. If some time have elapsed, more trouble is required; and not unfrequently no mental effort will serve to recall that which has gone from us. But is it therefore altogether gone? Can we confidently say this of anything that ever has been within the mind? What can seem more entirely passed away than a trivial conversation of years back, to which no particular interest attached then, which we never had any reason for remembering, and of which we might fairly say, that it never would again be recalled? Yet shall some unexpected turn in a road, some unusual conjunction of natural objects, some affection of some one of our senses, when we never expected it, bring back to us every word which passed in that trifling conversation. Where was that all these years? Clearly it was ours; not gone from us, though eluding the grasp of conscious recollection. Who has not heard of the first language of those who have left a foreign land of their birth in infancy, long and entirely forgotten, returning again in all its fluency during the delirium of fever? Where was that, while it was forgotten? Feebleness of the frame and of the brain brings tendency to forget; old age renders the mental grasp less active, less retentive; but who can tell whether, when the soul escapes from the worn-out machine, it may not possess, at once and without effort, that plenitude of memory of which we are treating, as a requisite for an account being given of the things done in the body?

Of the probability of our second condition

there might be even perhaps more reasonable doubt. That the whole record of time should be restored to the race of man, seems beyond all example or analogy. Yet even this may not be so. The divine inspiration by which the early historical books of Holy Scripture were written must at all events have been something of this kind. Matters unknown to the historian are related by his pen. Facts and precepts of which God alone was cognizant, are described by him. If we ask, how? The only Christian answer is, that God put them into his mind: opened the eyes of his perception, so that these facts came to him not through the outward senses, but by direct revelation. Thus it was that St. Paul too, as he expressly tells us, received from the Lord the Gospel history, which he himself had never witnessed; and we are led to expect something of this kind by that Apostle, when he speaks of the blessed state as one where we shall know even as we are known;

or as it should rather be, as we have long been known by God. There is no antecedent improbability in this intuitive consciousness of all matter of fact being that in which our perfect knowledge there will differ from our imperfect and partial knowledge here.

In conceiving and expecting our third condition, the possession of a perfect and unerring standard of right and justice, there is far less difficulty. I say nothing of the progress of Christian life, and maturity of gifts of the Holy Spirit, because I am speaking of that which must be common to all men; which must exist in order to the full condemnation of the lost, as well as to the entire fruition of God on the part of the blessed. But I will recall to you things of which we have all heard, and which some at least have witnessed; how sometimes in an instant, in the presence of solemn realities, the veil which hid truth and justice drops off, and a man sees things as they are. When death is known to be approaching, the meanest man's words put on oracular truth; the unforgiven one is called to the bedside, and the justice of the long-rejected plea is allowed. When death has called away a parent or a friend, then first our own disobedience, then first our own ingratitude and unkindness, puts on its true appearance; and generally when it is too late to do good, we see the good we might have done. All this seems to show us that in a man, down in the depths of a man, there does exist somewhere this true estimate which we want; and that it needs but the removal of all the obstacles which now stand in its way—the corruption of our flesh, and the seduction of the world—for it to be universally seen and recognized.

It does not then appear impossible, it does not even seem improbable, that these three conditions of the reality and justice of the final account may be one day fulfilled in every one of us. There has not appeared any reason why that solemn account may not in every case as completely condemn the sinner, and justify the servants of God,— why it may not in the sight of men and angels as entirely vindicate God's justice, and manifest forth his mercy, as any passage of Scripture assures us it will.

III.

PRACTICAL EFFECT ON LIFE.

In our last meditation we treated of man's final account—of the difficulties which seemed to lie about the conception of such final account as a reality, involving as it does the complete restoration of the memory of every minutest act, word, and thought; and, notwithstanding, the probability which exists from certain things which we find taking place in us even now, that such restoration will be furnished to us.

It was best to leave the practical part of my subject for another occasion. Let us take it up now. Let us consider what ought to be the effect on us of the expectation that our whole lives, in their minutest detail, will be again brought up before us, and made the subject of God's righteous judgment before men and angels.

And here we must begin with saying, undoubtedly the thought that it will be so is a strange and unaccustomed one. We are always in the habit of accounting that which is gone by to be really gone by, no more to return; or if we do expect to be called into judgment for our acts, it is thus that we shape the idea: that perhaps some of the greater things of our lives will be remembered for and against us, but that certainly all the lesser ones will not. We simply do not take them into account, but let them drift by, and forget them altogether. Now it may well be asked in the outset, does this want altering? Supposing it were possible, would it be desirable, that we should bear in mind every thought, word, and deed, or even that we should keep in mind very much more than we ordinarily do? Decidedly the answer must be, that it would not be desirable. No man could bear the burden of the irrevocable past resting on him in much greater weight than it already does. If memory were perfect, man would be utterly miserable. There would be no bounds to remorse, to self-accusation, to despair. All the sweet fallacies of hope would be powerless to rouse man to action. If all I have felt and said, all I have done and omitted to do, for one week, were to be enshrined imperishably in my memory, constituted as I now am, it would drive me to madness. No, depend on it God has done well to endow us frail and imperfect mortals with the faculty of forgetfulness. It may be doubted whether, of all our faculties and powers, any one has ministered so much to human happiness as this. For man is not meant to live in the past, but in the present, and in the future: in the present, in order to the future: in the future, that he may live well in the present.

According as a man has power of throwing himself intensely into the present, of forgetting what he has been, and remembering only what he is, and what he is to be,—in that proportion is he energetic, is he useful, does he impress the things that he does, or the age in which he lives, with reality, and work God's work, and do good in the world.

Enough of the past remains with all wise men, to take warning by; enough is ever present with all reasonable men, to take courage by; enough rests on the thoughts of all Christian men, to teach them to trust in God and distrust themselves. But no wise man, no reasonable man, no Christian man, will ever wish for more of the past to be constantly with him and pressing on his thoughts.

So that I do not think we need believe it to be a wrong thing, that we let the trivial thoughts, words, and deeds of the day thus slip away from us beyond recall. Still it is clear that, if they are all to be recalled some day, they ought by some means to be so cared for, that they may not at that day cause us shame and confusion.

"So live," says one, "as you will wish you had lived when you come to die: so live, that nothing in your life may be a terror to you when that life comes to be laid out before men and angels at the last day." Admirable advice: as good as it is obvious: but who can follow it? I suppose none but the most ignorant of himself, none but the most arrogant and conceited, will ever say that he has spent a day, or an hour, in accordance with this conventional good counsel. It is clearly in some other way than this, that we must set about our preparation for that day of account: not by being remiss in living purely, speaking charitably, thinking as responsible for our thoughts: God forbid: but by frankly acknowledging, that we cannot so live, as fearlessly to meet the Judge of all: by measuring, and confessing, the depth of our own unworthiness and shortcoming; and by at the same time diligently availing ourselves of whatever help

God has mercifully provided for us. For He has provided help for us, in this matter of our final account. He has not left us to accumulate guilt in His sight, hopeless of its ever being removed. It is most true, that this must be the case with man as he is by nature, and unassisted: it is true, that it will, alas! be the case with the holiest and best of us, even with all the means and appliances of God's grace within his reach: we shall all be found guilty in that day, and none can stand before Him. And yet, on the other hand, it is most true also, that there is such a thing as not fearing that final account: such a thing as being prepared for it, and looking to it even with calmness and assurance of hope. Let us see how this can be.

And in order to this, we must lay down one distinction very widely, which is far too often forgotten: a distinction, the due remembering of which lies at the very foundation of every Christian man's view of himself and his prospects. I mean the distinction between man as he is by nature, and man as he is under the grace of Christ. As we are by nature, we have abundantly seen that the mere thought of the great final account might well overpower us. It must be to us nothing short of absolute ruin and eternal death. And the mere natural man confesses this by his conduct. He endeavours to put the thought of that account far from him. He acts, he speaks, he thinks, as if it were never to come. He perhaps even affects, in spite of the continued testimony of conscience within him, to disbelieve it. However much he may repudiate the saying when alleged against him, the motto of his real practical life is "Let us eat and drink, for to-morrow we die, and are no more." And if this be not so, abject fear and contemptible superstition take the place of restlessness and unbelief. All kinds of vain expectations and unavailing satisfactions are invented, by which the terrors of the final account may be averted. Not that the craving for such refuge from its terrors is vain: it is one of the truest instincts of our nature, destined by Him who implanted it to lead us to happiness and peace: the mischief is, when men will not accept God's way to these blessed results, and will be setting up ways of their own invention: building, like those in Shinar of old, towers on this earth to reach to heaven.

But now let us look at the other side, and behold man in a state of grace. Such a contrast is fitting to the season of which we are writing; fitting to a time when we are close on the anniversary of His birth by whom grace and truth came in. Let us follow it out, simply and in detail, asking the meaning of the words which we use, as we use them. Man in a state of grace. And what is grace? Grace means simply the *Divine favour*—God's good pleasure restored to the rebellious race of men, and with that, all the means of serving God, and further, pleasing God, and being at peace with God, and rejoicing in God, and becoming like God, and finally attaining unto God in everlasting bliss. All this is comprehended in that word *grace;* all this belongs to man as in the state of grace. And now we come to the plain belief of Christ's universal Church: to that glorious subject which the present season is about to introduce in all its renewed joy before us. This grace was brought in, came about, by means of One Man: and that man is God incarnate in our flesh—Jesus Christ, the eternal Son of God, and the suffering, triumphant, and glorified Son of man. And the Church, the body of men which receives Him as the author and bringer in of this grace and favour of God, believes this about Him and about its members: that those who are admitted, by the ordinance which He appointed, into visible membership with Him, from having been born in sin and being children of wrath, do become children of grace: from being merely members of this human race, children of earthly parents, and inheritors of God's wrath, which rests on our guilty state, become members of Christ, children of God, and inheritors of the kingdom of heaven. This is our belief, taught us when children, adopted consciously by us at our confirmation, acted on by us as often as we meet together in church, or approach God in any way. We are His people, reconciled to Him in Christ, bound to His service, upheld by His Spirit, looking for His mercy unto eternal life.

Now it is time to ask, how does it stand in our case with regard to this great final account? Shall we escape it? Certainly not. When St. Paul used the words "We must all appear (or more properly " must all be made manifest ") before the judgment-seat of Christ," he was speaking of himself and those to whom he was writing, all of whom were in this state of grace. We shall not escape the final account. But what says our Lord himself respecting it, and his believing people? "He that heareth my word, and believeth on Him that sent Me, hath everlasting life, and shall not come into condemnation (rather, shall not come into judgment, shall not incur the peril, the risk of being unfavourably judged); but is passed from death unto life." What a wonderful thing is this! His believing ones are in no danger of condemnation in that great final account: they shall be borne blameless throughout it, notwithstanding their own utter unworthiness and inability to endure its searching questions. And how is this? By what marvellous arrangement? How, consistently with God's justice? How, consistently with the Judge of all the earth doing right? The tale is an old one to us, but let it ever be a fresh and living one in its bearing and influence on us. The Son of God who became Son of man, died: died, bearing on Him the sins of the race of man; put away sin by the sacrifice of Himself: and they who are united to Him by a true and living faith, have entered into and put on this sinlessness of His, this triumph of His, this glory of His. They live, not to themselves, but to Him. Not their own life, but His; not for their own profit, but for the glory of His infinite love and grace in giving Himself for them and saving them. And now do we inquire, for what shall those be judged and called in question who are members of Christ's Church? Do we ask, when judgment shall begin at the house of God, what shall be its subject and aim? What in that day shall distinguish one baptized person from another, so that one shall be an accepted guest at the marriage supper of the Lamb, and the other thrust out into utter darkness? What but this; the question as to the reality and living power in each of us of that faith in Christ into which we were all admitted at our baptism? One man believed in his Saviour as a living and loving Master, ever by him, ever upholding him, ever requiring his love and simple obedience: a thousand imperfections marred his service, a hundred falls into sin might be laid to his charge, but they have not been his will, they have been wrought against his consent, in spite of his watchful care. There is One who shall answer for him, One on whom all his sins and imperfections are laid, and he is safe; safe in the shadow of the Rock; safe in the rest given to the weary and heavy-laden: safe, though he has erred and strayed like a sheep that is lost, in the arms of the Chief Shepherd, who died to ransom the flock. And then another, baptized like him, a member of the same Church, and partaker of the same privileges, never made these things a reality to himself; went on through life hearing of Christ, talking of Christ, doubting, it may be, about Christ, or not caring about Him at all: and he shall be shut out and condemned, because he hath not believed on the only begotten Son of God: hath not served Him, never cared for Him, or for waking up in his likeness. Here is the difference between man and man in the state of grace: here is the preparation for the awful account of that day. If all my sins rise behind me dark as the tempest in that day, and if I have held by Christ, lived on Christ, striven by Christ's grace to obey Him, and to be like Him, then all is well. He will be my refuge and strength, and my exceeding great reward. But if while professing to belong to Him, I have not cared for Him or his word, have let my belief in Him be a mere sound and a fable, never penetrating my heart—then will the account of that day overwhelm me with everlasting confusion. May we look on the two —may we make our choice, and prepare accordingly for what must ere long come upon us all.

IV.

NO CHANGE IN NATURE?

ONE form of unbelief, very prevalent in our days, founds its distrust of religion on the permanence of the laws of nature. It can perhaps be hardly more accurately described than in the words of St. Peter (2 Pet. iii. 4), as saying, "Where is the promise of His coming? For since the fathers fell asleep, all things are as they were from the beginning of the creation." The laws of nature, it is alleged, are fixed and permanent; and we know of no instances in which they have been interfered with. Therefore, these persons somewhat inconsequently add, they never have been, and never shall be, interfered with.

Now I am not going at present to complain of the inconsequence of this inference, that, because a thing has not happened within our experience, therefore it never can have happened, and never shall happen; but I wish to meet those who thus reason on another ground; to examine into the truth of their chief axiom, this supposed permanence of the present state of things, and see whether we can entirely rely upon it in a matter so important as this, where our eternal hopes and interests are concerned.

But before I do so, let me set before you a distinct idea as to what this form of unbelief amounts to; how far it goes, and what, if consistent, it proposes to itself.

To deny all interference with nature, is to deny that there is such a thing as what we call the supernatural. This denial the advocates of the view which I am describing distinctly avow. There is absolutely no supernatural, they say. In other words—and they have no right to shrink from it—there is no God. For if there be a God, who made Nature and ordained her laws, it is clearly within his power to set aside those laws and act without them when He pleases: and who shall say when He may be so pleased? So that the consideration that all things are as they were from the beginning of the creation, not only suggests to them a doubt of Christ's second coming, but causes them to deny that He ever came at all, in the sense in which we believe Him to have come, as God incarnate in the nature of man: it leads them to deny all His miracles and all His prophecies, and while they profess to admire Him as a teacher of morals and as an example of truth and love, they must, if they are consistent with themselves, also hold

Him to have been an impostor and deceiver: because He plainly did set up claim to miraculous powers, and to the gift of prophecy. So that the real tendency of the kind of unbelief of which I speak, is not, as its most popular expounder would have us believe, to clear up the character of Jesus, and set Him before us as a great teacher and example; but it is, to put Him altogether out of the number of the world's benefactors, and His teaching out of our regard as any pattern for our moral obedience. One who condescended to impose on others by pretended miracles, cannot be worth anything as a teacher of truth. Even if this were not so (though this is what is actually held by them), one who lived, spoke, wrought, and died, in an intense belief of the supernatural, cannot be good for much as a guide for men who know that the supernatural is impossible.

This kind of unbelief then tends directly to rob us of one whom we have been accustomed to regard as our Redeemer, our

Teacher, and our Example: one whom every Christian believes to be at this moment at God's right hand in heaven, waiting, in our glorified nature, till all things are put under His feet; and then about to come in person to judge the quick and dead. The great exploit which the atheist forerunner of revolutionary France demanded, the wiping out of Him whom Christians worship, has thus, it would seem, been accomplished a century after, by a brilliant and accomplished writer of the same nation, who professes to set his character in its true light, and claims to admire and love Him even more than we do. And it is to be feared that this writer does not by any means stand alone. A habit is becoming sadly prevalent in educated circles, and especially where the greatest amount of our national intelligence dwells, in the middle class of our countrymen, of speaking of this world and its facts — things present, things palpable—as certainties; and of all beyond it, religion, with its facts and promises, as uncertain, and the realm of legend and fable. And if one questions the ground of such an estimate, it is generally found to be the very one of which I have been speaking,— that the course of nature is one and unalterable; and that, as far as we can see, the supernatural is impossible.

It is high time, then, that we should examine into this foundation axiom of our modern school of unbelief. "All things are as they were from the beginning of the creation. Nature never changes: never returns on her footsteps: any interference with her course is simply inconceivable." Now is this so? Let us go abroad into Creation and see. If permanence means anything, it may be applied to the face of the earth as we behold it. Scripture gives us a true representation of what men feel about this, when it speaks of the "everlasting hills." Hill and dale are, as it were, terms of the covenant by which man holds the earth. Now what is the testimony of the hills as to the permanence of all things as they were from the beginning? Let us dig into the first hill we come to, and what shall we find? In some cases, the records of a former world, with animals and plants of its own: in others, masses of primitive rock which has broken up from beneath in a state of fusion: in others again, vast accretions of *débris*, brought thither by some unknown force, all record of which has long since passed away. Look at the bare face of any limestone cliff or stone quarry, and surely all faith in the permanence of the present state of things, with the quiet working of its ordinary laws, must be at an end. I speak not now of all that animal and vegetable matter imbedded in those strata whose lines we can trace in the rock: but what power upheaved those strata themselves, some, as their very nature testifies, once lying horizontal for hundreds of feet in thickness and hundreds of miles in extent? What ordinary force now in operation, and to be looked for from day to day, uplifted the vast chains of the Alps, the Andes, the Himalayas? Grant that it was but an exaggeration of forces now in operation: and what has the opponent gained? Nothing but this: this at the worst, and this at the least: that at some time in the earth's history, an exertion of those forces took place sufficient to overthrow the whole existing order of things; sufficient to clear large portions of the earth's surface of their animal and vegetable inhabitants; sufficient to divide the sea from the land, and to re-distribute oceans and continents; sufficient to alter conditions of climates; to bring cold, where tropical heat once prevailed, and again, moderate temperature, where once were vast seas of ice. No record exists of any such change in our time, or in the time of our race. Had our race dwelt then on earth, it must have been extinguished in those general convulsions: and that it did not then exist is plain; for among the more ancient wrecks of the conditions which preceded this present one, neither man himself, nor the animals which now dwell with man on the earth, can be found at all.

Now I would ask our opponents: of what kind were such convulsions as these? Granted, as I said before, that they may have been brought about by the exaggerated agency of laws still operating; what has now become of such exaggerated agencies? Why are they not continually breaking forth from time to time? Why have they slumbered, I will not say for 6,000 years, because that would be to assume a period which the unbeliever might not be disposed to concede,— but for 2,500, the shortest limit which, I suppose, the most sceptical will put to the historic period? What is the worst earthquake that history has ever recorded, compared with the convulsion to which the most ordinary range of hills owes its existence? And couple this with the fact, that after each such convulsion we find a new order of things, as testified by the existing remains: new animals, new plants, new conditions of climate; and at a certain time in the series, when the globe has become as it were prepared for his habitation, our race appears, peopling the earth and replenishing it: what man with the exercise of common sense can look upon such a set of phenomena, and not infer that the existing order of nature has been from time to time broken in upon by a will above nature? Whether that will acted in each case according to, or by the suspending of the ordinary laws of nature, is, I conceive, of little consequence: give us a personal will above nature, and I am content.

And if such be the testimony of the earth itself, surely it is corroborated by that of the earth's history. Where in its progress do we find any guarantee for the permanence of the existing order of things? Set every hedge you will about any given dynasty or form of government; advance as far as you will in social and moral progress; make security and continued peace next to certain; remove every element of discontent and discord: and then warrant the permanence of a dynasty, of a government, of a nation's tranquillity. The morning may witness the boast, and the evening may set in revolution and blood: the occupant of the throne may be an exile, the stable government overthrown, neighbour set against neighbour and brother against brother, with a ferocity unknown in previous history. Sudden change thus befalls human affairs, in spite of all man's precaution. Fixed laws are not to be calculated on here, any more than in nature. They operate, it is true; but not without certain rude interruptions which, happening often without assignable cause, shatter the fair hopes of those who had calculated on permanence. Here, as in the other case, the inference drawn by mankind ever has been, that there is a Power above and outside the fabric of human society, fashioning its similitudes according to His will.

And even more strikingly is this seen to be so, if we regard, not only sudden interruptions of the working of the mental and social laws by which our race is regulated, but also the gradual progress which the world has made under the operation of those laws themselves. Let any one cast but the most cursory glance over man's history, and he can hardly fail to perceive that the general character of its course has been, good coming to man in spite of man: great schemes of ambition overruled for good: evil warded off from nations, not by, but contrary to, their most earnest wishes: the greatest calamities turned into the greatest blessings: and looking at the world as a whole, a gradual upward progress, quite unaccountable, if man were left to himself, but then only capable of explanation, if we suppose One who cares for man to be wielding the destinies of man.

Let us change the scene once more. Let us look each on his own history in life. Are all things here as they were from the beginning? Has our outer or our inner life gone on by a fixed rule, so that we could calculate it from year to year; so that we could say, I know what it shall be, and none shall interfere with it? Who can say this? Has it not rather been always so led, that we have felt it has not been in ourselves to direct our ways; so that we have trembled as we looked forward, not knowing what might be His will, in whose hands we knew our destinies to be? Do we not all feel that any day might bring loss of health, loss of friends, loss of worldly means, loss of reason, loss of life? And is not this feeling a very instinct of our humanity? Is not the denial of its truth a denial of the very conditions of our own being? In our nature is implanted a consciousness of the supernatural: and he who pronounces the supernatural to be impossible, is, while he does so, denying his own convictions.

And notice again what I said before—that this argument of unbelief, to be good for anything, must be good for everything. Unless it can prevail to the exclusion of the supernatural from everything, it is absolutely worthless. If there be any Power watching over man, then much more over that lower nature and inferior world of which man is constituted head and chief. If matter was created at all, then He who created it framed the laws which now regulate it, and can suspend them, or undo His creation, if it be His will. If any link in the chain is loose, the whole will give way. And I believe that we have shewn, that there are links loose in many places: that whether we look at the course of nature, or at the world's history, or at that of the individual, we do not find any reason to doubt, but every reason to infer with certainty, that there is One who ruleth all of them, who is above nature, and whose doings, if ever He is pleased to interfere with nature, must be called strictly supernatural.

So that, these things being so, I cannot feel, and I cannot imagine how any man with ordinary common sense can feel, the slightest difficulty in the mere receiving as a fact, of the exertion of power suspending or setting aside the laws of nature, even though nothing of the kind may have been witnessed by ourselves, or within our own times or those of our fathers. Many reasons may be conceived why at certain periods of the world's history such manifestations should be suspended. The Creation has been such a manifestation,—renewed, it would appear, at periods widely distant, when different races of beings, now extinct, were produced,—and for the last time, on the calling into life of the race which now inhabit our world.

But, creation being once accomplished, and the laws of organic being fixed, the world was left during the rest of each period respectively to obey those laws for the most part without interference. And why should this not also be the case in the world of man's spirit, and of that knowledge of God upon which it is to be nurtured for immortality? At the first opening of the dispensation of grace and truth by Jesus Christ, supernatural interference was absolutely necessary. God cannot make a special revelation of Himself without departing from the ordinary course of nature—the very terms imply it. But that revelation once made, and established by His own interference as His truth, the Church is left to obey the new laws, so to speak, of the organised being thus impressed upon her.

Besides, another mistake, or rather another set of mistakes, is made by those whose views we have been controverting; the habit of confounding together two things entirely distinct;

that which is contrary to nature, and that which is merely obedience to a higher law of nature instead of a lower. Let me make my meaning plain by an example. That a dead corpse, laid in the tomb, should in the ordinary course reorganise itself and become quickened, and after a certain time come out of the tomb a living body, is absolutely contrary to nature. No provisions are made in the ordinary course of things for such a process; nay, all is against it; and we may with certainty say that it never has happened, and never will happen. But for the God of nature, or any one having authority from the God of nature, to stand by that tomb and summon the dead corpse, and then for that corpse to come forth a living body, reorganised and quickened, this is not contrary to nature; this is in obedience to nature's first and highest law—the supreme will of the Creator. And for us to say it is not likely that the God of nature would ever do this, or authorize any one to do it, is simply folly and presumption, seeing that we cannot prescribe to Him His conduct, nor say what He may deem it fit to do.

Now, transferring these considerations to the great subject of this season, and using them as a reply to the question, " Where is the promise of His coming?" two or three thoughts occur to us which may be profitably dwelt upon.

First of all, we see from the testimony of the earth itself, that former periods have had their beginning and their end, each accompanied by interruptions, more or less violent, to the preceding or the existing order of things. It is, then, according to analogy, that this our period should have its end also.

Next, the entire evidence, derived from the same phenomena, is in favour of the view, that the whole course of these periods has been one of upward progress. This last period, and, as far as we can ascertain, none before it, has been distinguished by the existence upon our globe of a sentient race of beings, who have subdued it to their purposes, and have been endowed with faculties of the highest order. Is it anything unreasonable to suppose, that inasmuch as this race have had opened to them the knowledge of their Creator, and implanted in their minds the desire after Him, and the hope of enjoying Him in immortality, He should be especially present with them, at their origin, at each of His manifestations of Himself to them, and, above all, at the destined end of their career, when His purposes shall have been accomplished respecting them? Again, if it be His purpose, as we believe it is, Himself to stand at the latter day upon the earth, and to be seen by us all, and to call the dead out of their graves, I cannot see that this will be any violation, or even any interruption, of the laws of nature, if only we understand that term aright. No violation. To him indeed who only looks on this earth and what he sees here, it may appear to violate the established laws of things. But this is only because he sees but a few of them, and his views are confined to those few. And again, in the true sense of the word, it will be no interruption either; because, not only for the ordinary process, but also for this the final consummation, was provision made in the purposes of the All-wise and All-provident: this was itself part of the destined course, and interwoven into the series of causes and effects foreseen from the beginning.

So that, as it seems to me, there is nothing in any such considerations of the regularity and permanence of nature, which need affect us Christian believers in respect of any of the articles of our faith. Whenever, and by whomsoever such thoughts are pressed upon us,—whether by avowed opponents, or by disguised pretenders to admiration of the character and course of our Master, our duty is one and the same. Prove all things. Be not agitated, be not provoked to wrath. Revile not: give no opportunity by weakness to the eager and wary foe. Take his arguments, sift them carefully, make every allowance, deal liberally and large-heartedly; by this you will lose nothing. And when this has been done, it will ever be found that error has been dissipated and truth made clearer.

Where is the promise of His coming? Here, written on the face of the earth, read on the arch of the heavens; here, written in the record of His manifestation of Himself to man; here, laid up in our hearts, bright at the end of all our thoughts, and warming and quickening all our course of action. Where is it, seeing that all things remain as they were? Yes, we reply, all things remain; and more than the questioner thinks of. For among them remain His unfailing word, His abiding presence, His unwearied ordinances. He said He would be with us all the days, even to the end of the world. The days are not yet past, nor has He ceased to be among us; we still believe in the end, when not His Spirit only, but His glorified Countenance, shall shine on us for ever.

ON CREATION.

I.

THE subject of *Creation*, as it presents itself to the religious mind in connection with our actual circumstances and habits of thought, is one which, it seems to me, we may profitably meditate on. It is especially important in our days to take an account of the great truths which we profess to believe: to put them side by side with what we know and daily feel: and thus to keep ourselves ever in a condition, so to speak, of familiar intercourse with them; that we may not have first to make their real acquaintance when we ought to be defending them against the faith's enemies, or making use of them in our own hour of need.

GOD CREATED THE HEAVENS AND THE EARTH. —This is our central fact. First, let us look on it *as a fact*. It is in every one's mouth; but what do we mean by it, and how does it look when we realize it? Regard it which way we will, it is a thing entirely removed from our experience, and passing our comprehension. For what do we know of Creation, as an act? All that is ever *made* here on earth, is nothing but a new arrangement of previously existing material; and this is true, not only of that which *we* make, but of all outward objects of the senses that *God* makes now, in this existing state of things. This globe, in all probability, does not now contain one particle of matter more than it did when it was first created. Animals and plants have sprung up and decayed, and their material has passed into the substance of the earth, and thence into new animals and plants, and so on through the series of ages. But there has been only one work of material *Creation*, properly and strictly so called; and that is the act related in these words, " In the beginning God created the heavens and the earth." This act is entirely distinct from most of those that follow it in that wonderful story in the first chapter of Genesis. For most of those that follow are not so much acts of creation as of arrangement, and endowment with power of production out of given material. All of these are *God's* acts— acts of almighty power and infinite wisdom, by which life may originate and may be supported; but, except in a sense which I am not yet considering, they are not like this first one. And what is this act? One of which, as I said, we have no conception: which as far surpasses us as any other of the ways and acts of God: it is the calling matter into being *out of nothing*. Let us try to make this real to ourselves. Our imagination must, in order to this, traverse back far above the earliest period known even to the vast inferences of geological science; even to the time when God was alone in the void universe, and nothing besides: an infinite Spirit inhabiting Eternity. Perhaps we can form some conception approaching to the truth of this, strange as the conception may be. But it is the next step which appears so utterly to baffle us. Suddenly or gradually—for this makes no difference to our difficulty or to the resulting fact—at the command of God, matter comes into existence. Vast masses of solid material are, where absolutely nothing was before: are, without having been transported from elsewhere: come into existence out of nothing. Am I not right in saying that such a thing utterly and entirely passes our power of comprehension, and all obvious examples and analogies of which we know? We believe it: but we are obliged to stop when we get close up to the fact, so to speak, and to pass from inquiry to acceptance; from reason and imagination, and all that we ever saw or knew or heard of, to faith, and faith only. "Through faith we understand that the worlds were framed by the word of God, so that things which are seen were not made of things which do appear."

Here, then, we stand at the same point where we stood in our former meditations in the same strain respecting the Lord's coming, and our own final account. The great thing which we believe is one only to be believed, not to be assured to us by any power of our own to comprehend it. All the arguments about God's benevolent designs in creation, His wonderful arrangements for the well-being and good of His creatures, do not apply to this point at all: for this point is, not the arrangement, but the bringing into existence, of the materials of this and of all the worlds.

The ancient heathen could reason as touchingly and as convincingly about the benevolent designs of the Creator, as have our own Christian writers; but the heathen never knew, as a doctrine of their religion, this wonderful fact of the creation of matter out of nothing. With them, matter was eternal; and the Creator only used the material which was ready to His hand.

But now let us take the same course which we did on those other occasions, and let us see whether our faith in the fact, that God in the beginning created the heavens and the earth, may not find present confirmation from what we behold going on around us day by day. We said that we see no such thing now as creation of new matter. In the natural world such a phenomenon is unknown. But is it in the spiritual? When the existence of each of us began, what happened? As far as the body is concerned, no more than what we have already spoken of. The body is composed of, the body is nourished by, materials previously existing in the world. But is this so with the mental part of us? is it so with the spiritual part? It is true that, to a certain extent, even this is affected by descent from minds and spirits previously existing. But it is also true that there is no way of accounting for the personality and responsibility of the human soul, without believing every individual spirit to have come immediately from God's creative hand. The creation of each human being was as completely a calling into existence out of nothing, as the creation of the material of a world. Let us go back in our thoughts here, as we did in that case before, to a time when there was no created rational being: to the first creative act by which sentient being began. Where, a moment since, all was blank, there sprang into life a soul, with all its powers, all its responsibilities, all its sympathies: but above all these, and including all these, with its personal being, existing side by side with Him who called it into life. If we compare these two together, the creation of a mass of matter and the creation of a living soul, far above our comprehension as both of them are, shall we not necessarily confess that to create a spirit seems to us, when we ponder on the matter, the greater and more marvellous work? And yet this is going on before our eyes every day. Tell me not that God's creative acts in the spiritual world are ever carried on in subordination to certain natural laws. This makes no difference to my argument: my argument is, that we daily witness the creation of spirits: we constantly see before us a living, thinking, responsible soul, where but just now there was none. The fact is there, and we cannot deny it; we can understand it as little as we can understand the other; but here it is, continually going on. Why then should we feel it against us to believe in God's having called the material of the worlds out of nothing, seeing that He daily calls immortal souls out of nothing?

It is plain that I might have sought my example further down in animal creation. The life that moves in the brute animal is not any necessary result of the combination of the particles of matter of which the animal consists. Man might put together those particles with all the skill in his power, but there would be no life. Every life of animal, every life of any organised matter, is a creation of God. God is ever creating,—as well as ever using, in His marvellous wisdom, materials which He has already created.

Now I have as yet been meditating on the Creator, and on creation, as those might meditate who simply believed in one Supreme Ruler of the universe. But be it never forgotten that we, as Christians, have other and more satisfactory grounds to go on than the mere Deist, as to the process and the intent of creation. We know that the making of the worlds was not an act of power only, nor was it only an act of divine benevolence toward those who might inhabit them. It had a further and a far higher purpose than these. Indeed, if it had not, the charge might not unfairly be brought, that neither of the aims of the Creator has been accomplished; that there is not universal happiness and well-being in the world which we know; nor is it a perfect display of His supreme power; but that His benevolent designs have been marred by sin, and misery, and death, and His power thwarted by an adversary. Now I do not mean to say that Christianity has enabled us to solve the whole mystery of sin, and misery, and death; nor of the irruption of that adversary into God's world. There will be still, even when we have all its revelations in their fulness, much in these things that will be painfully incomprehensible, and that will require faith to arrive at, and yield to faith only; but I do mean to say, that Christianity has given us the master-key to all such difficulties, and that we may well believe, from the number of closed doors which it already opens, that those to which we have not access, and those whose locks refuse at present to yield to our weak hands, will eventually give way to it. And how has that master-key been furnished? What do we Christians know about Creation, more than the mere unaided reasoner, more than the mere Deist knows?

In answering this question, I shall assume the great doctrines of our faith: I shall not stay to confirm them, but simply take them for granted: wishing to inquire, not now into them, but into that which by means of them we know of the world about us, more than they do who receive them not. We believe then that the great Creator of the universe, the One God over all, has from eternity existed in three divine Persons—Father, Son, and Holy Spirit—co-eternal together and coequal. And Holy Scripture has not left us ignorant, as regards the process of creation, of the parts borne in it by those several Persons of the Holy Trinity. The Father, doing all things after the counsel of His own will, created the world by the Son, who is His Word, the expression of His power and love; and the Holy Spirit, the Lord and the Giver of life, wrought in this Creation, to the production of light, and life, and order, and being, and perfection. And all this we know was done for a gracious and glorious purpose. The material world was created to subserve the spiritual. Man was created the lord of the material world, that by means of his use of it, and of his own spiritual faculties, as served by his senses, he might rise into participation of the nature and blessedness of God himself. And we further know that, in order to this glorification of God in and by His human creatures, trial, and conflict, and sorrow, and suffering, and death, are steps necessary and inevitable. We know that these were originally introduced by man's own choice and fault, that choice and fault being brought about by the action of temptation on his will, which was necessarily created free to stand and free to fall. Again, I do not mean to say that our understanding can master every step of this; but I am bringing it all forward, as that which we read and believe, and in order to see what light it throws upon the process and the aim of Creation.

Now when we take these things into account, it seems very plain to me that we must take into account a good deal more, before we shall properly appreciate this aim of Creation. Think of the words, "the Lamb slain from before the foundation of the world." When I read such a Scripture sentence as this, am I wrong in saying or writing, as I have often done, that Creation is only a part of Redemption? It was God's design from eternity to bring the sons of men to a sharing of His glory by the elevation of their spiritual nature. Not, observe, by any act of His power; not to create at once beings who might sit upon thrones near to Himself; but to create spiritual, responsible beings, who might, by action on their own spirits, aided by His grace, become renovated, become elevated, become glorified, even till they should ascend up where He is, and sit down with Him on His throne. Now for this purpose He made the worlds; made the worlds by that blessed Son of His, who was from eternity destined to be the Head by Lordship over all created things; the Head, by actual participation, of the great human family; the Captain in the mighty conflict; the Lamb slain as a sacrifice for sin; the first-born from the dead, and the Conqueror of Death; the Prince and Saviour of His people. For Him and for His, God created all this which we see around us. For Christ, and Christ's Church it is, that nature exists; that the laws of nature have been established. For us, and for our bliss, and for our glorification, soul and body, it is, that the sun rules the day, and the moon the night; that the earth buds and blooms, and brings forth her fruit; that a thousand inferior races live and move around us; that seasons pass onward, and times recur, and all the vast fabric of creation works onward to a final consummation. For "all things are ours: whether life or death, or things present or things to come, all are ours; and we are Christ's, and Christ is God's."

So then Creation to the Christian—and, allow me to say, to the Christian alone—has its voice and its meaning, though not everywhere actually and at present understood, yet speaking so as to shew the way to the understanding of it all another day. Of this great and blessed view of Creation, the unbeliever knows nothing. It is to him simply a painful riddle. He weighs misery which he does see against happiness which he does not see, and he is confounded by the comparison. It all seems blank, and aimless, and inexplicable. He sees not why God the

Beneficent should have made man to suffer, should have made the animals to suffer, should have allowed the clear skies to be dashed with storm, and the bright flowers to wither with blight, and strength to pass into weakness, and power to be baffled, and beauty to decay, and promise to issue in disappointment. Neither do *we* see *all* this: but there hath sprung up to us light in the darkness; there is in the cloud the bow of the Covenant, and we are assured that, though we cannot see all, all is well: that in the end God will be justified, and everything that He hath made will be shewn to be very good.

From this let us carry away the lesson, that we ought as Christians to be very careful to keep Creation, in our thoughts, in its right place. Second let it ever be, not first: subordinate to our holy faith, not overruling it. From neglecting this, much unbelief arises. A man regards the world about him as his reality, and his religion as mere matter of shifting opinion, turned about hither and thither by things around him, by converse, and by books. Now this ought to be just the other way. Our religion is our reality; it alone is certain. It may be that God's creation, and God's providence, may cast light upon it from time to time; but, in the main, by it must they be interpreted, not it by them. We know that God made the heavens and the earth, and all that therein is: we know that He made them by His Eternal Son, and the agency of His blessed Spirit: we know that He made them to manifest the wonders of His Love by victory in the conflict with Evil: we know that He who by His Death and Resurrection won for us this victory, upholds all creation by His power. These are our facts, and on these everything else depends; all our outward knowledge, all science, all wholesome research, all that we can say or be persuaded about outward things: from these great truths of our faith is their truth derived, and by their subordinate truth shall those great truths shine clearer and be better known.

Thus let us think of Creation, and it will be to us, not a painful and dispiriting ænigma, but a portion of the ways of Him whom to know truly is life eternal.

II.

Creation then, material made out of nothing by God, is all around us; and we are part of it ourselves: we see it, we hear it, we touch it: and our own bodies are in these respects acted on by it, as it is acted on by them. And all this is a portion of our Christian life, in the wondrous scheme of Redemption. For the carrying out of that scheme, as we saw before, Creation was called into existence.

Now belonging to this part of our subject, our present connection with Creation, there are some considerations full of wonder and mystery. We, our personal and immortal part, are at present inseparably bound up with created matter.

By means of it we live, and move, and have our being. If it receives injury, we suffer: if its waste is not daily repaired, our spirits sink, and our vital energies decay. And this is wonderful to think of, even in itself—to think that such a thing ever should be so at all. But it is still more wonderful to think of, when viewed in this light. At any moment any one of us may be called on to quit this connection, at present so necessary, with created matter. I who write, using organs now consisting of created matter, may, before an hour has passed, become entirely unconnected with any created *matter* whatever : may go forth into space, or— for even such an expression is too material— simply exist, as a disembodied spirit. Two things are wonderful here. First, that such a thing should be : next, that it should be able to take place in an instant, and without preparation.

That it should be. As we are now, everything depends on the state of the body, everything depends on the outward conditions around the body. In racking pain, in deadly faintness, in unconquerable fatigue, of what avail is the vigour of the spirit? How dependent for exertion are we on the firmness of the step, on the steadiness of the hand, on the correctness of the eye, on the powers of the brain to collect and concentrate thought! And even if all these were in vigour, yet if external conditions are unfavourable, all will be in vain. If the earth were shaken, and the ground beneath us were unsteady: if the light of day were withdrawn: if the materials of our work were wanting to us, or the proper shelter in which that work should be carried on: all our own powers would be unable to effect that for which they are calculated. We are, in this present state, the slaves of matter. That we should exist in entire disconnection from it, is at first sight almost inconceivable. And when we come to join to this, that an instant only is the boundary of two states so apparently inconsistent with one another;

that at one moment the soul is bound in the fetters of sense, nay, entirely held down by them in powerless and utter prostration,—and at the next moment is absolutely free from them and existing independently, the wonder and difficulty of the fact do indeed seem to be greater than we are able to surmount in our imagination.

Still, let us view it by the light of other considerations, as undoubted, and forming part of our every-day experience. We can hardly speak or act, without bearing testimony that things really are as it has just now appeared so wonderful that they should be. How do we regard things about us? How do we regard our own bodies, with which we are thus bound up? Do we ever look on them as part of ourselves? As far as I know, never on any occasion. As to things about us, palpably and clearly, not. We migrate from home to home: we loosen and we bind attachments: and, however some persons may be disposed to cling to the same circumstances and places, we are quite unable to conceive that any one should ever come to imagine external things necessary to his own existence. And even so is it with our own very bodies: they are our possessions, but they are not ourselves. However near portions of them may be to the apparent seat of life, and essential to its maintenance, we never for a moment treat or speak of them as if they were ourselves. Injury or loss of them will be sure to dissolve that life: yet we ever call them *ours*, not *us*. Nay, sometimes, in their utter disorganisation and destruction, the spirit asserts its mastery: and it is seen, amidst the crash of the fatal accident, or from the all but finished decay of the wasted frame, that matter is not man: that man is not bound to matter.

As we proceed, we have other analogies suggested to us which illustrate our subject. Thought—what is it? Clearly, nothing that is, or that is in itself dependent upon, matter. Yet are we entirely beholden to matter for our power of communicating thought. It is spoken—we receive it through the agitation of the air by sound: it is written—we receive it by the stains made by some colouring matter on paper. Yet that which is received in each case is as entirely distinct from any sounds or any written characters, as the spirit is from the body. It is a spiritual thing; and, when once received into the mind, subsists there independently of any material medium. It may be conveyed to the deaf by signals—to the blind by touch: one mind may make use of matter in various ways to communicate with another mind, but the communication is of that which is of itself not material. Nay, in all the purer and higher processes of thought, when we work inwardly by the laws of our reasoning faculties,—be it on our own spiritual life, or on the nature of God, or on the laws of abstract science, or on any other purely mental subject that we meditate, then for the time, however liable such thought may be to be disturbed by things around us, we are, as nearly as the case admits of, actually putting ourselves into the state of freedom from the body, and anticipating our condition when this shall really have come to pass.

So that, though it may be to us, in our present state, a most wonderful thing that we should exist as spirits and be conscious without the body, yet from much that now passes we see that it is not inconceivable, but that in our purest and highest moods we are continually approaching that condition.

I said just now, that the suddenness of the transition to the disembodied state was a strange and a wonderful thing. We cannot indeed tell by what gradual steps the spirit, set free from the body, may be permitted or empowered to realize its new condition: but of this we are sure, that however this may be, all those steps must be taken in the disembodied, not in the corporeal state. If we do not hold a sleep of the soul (and I suppose no thinking Christian possibly can hold this), there must be an instantaneous passage, in most men's case, from consciousness in the embodied state to consciousness in the disembodied state. And this has ever to my mind been the strangest thing about death; the consideration of that moment of transition—that new awakening to consciousness in the world of spirits.

But again, I do not see anything in it which may not be: anything of which we have not example at least approaching in kind to the reality, though very short of it in degree. For what is our awakening each morning of our lives? or to come even nearer, what is awakening from a dream to real life? Are not these, is not especially this latter, an instantaneous exchange of one state for another? And this is done every day without any violent shock, as tranquilly and naturally as we pass from one subject of thought to another.

Now in coming to the main portion of that which concerns us, the use of Creation about us in our present state, what we have been but now considering will be of great use to us; and we must carry it somewhat further, to get at its full use.

The disembodied state is not our final state. We are again to be joined to the body: we are again to be joined to the *same* body with which we were before united. It will not be of the same particles of substance; but that is not necessary to its identity; for its substance has been changed over and over again, while it remained the same body here. It will probably not be the exact actual body, even in appearance, which we bore at any time during our earthly pilgrimage: but it will be the same body. It will have lost its mortality, its liability to decay, to pain, to weakness,—possibly all its traces of all these; but not its identity. Created matter it will still be, and it will be in a world of created matter. Thus much I am obliged to say in anticipation of the next portion of my subject: and I shall anticipate it no more. Thus much was necessary, to show the use of this world of matter which lies about us.

And I must also look back for a moment on what we shewed before. We tried to make it clear, that the world was made for Christ, and for Christ's Church. It was a part of the great and glorious scheme of Redemption, to lead the sons of God, through trial, and through increase of knowledge, and through a course of holy obedience, all in a material body, and surrounded with material circumstances.

Well then, if we ask the question, what purpose does Creation at present serve to us who are parts of it and surrounded by it?—the first and most obvious answer will be, that it is our appointed sphere of trial, and condition of preparation for our glorious final state. Now this may sound a commonplace thing to say: but I very much doubt whether it enters one half as much into men's thoughts of themselves, and of the world about them, as it ought to do. When we say, Creation is our sphere of trial, what do we mean? Consider how wide the words ought to extend, if they have really any meaning at all. God has given us senses: God has given us created matter for those senses to act on, and to be acted on by. The objects with which we are thus brought into contact are innumerable. Have we a right to say that any, even the meanest of those objects, bears no part in the trial and preparation of us for our final state? Of all that the eye can behold, and the ear can hear, and the hand can touch, and the tongue can taste, is there anything so mean, as to be altogether without part in acting for good or for harm on the immortal spirit? The question is easily answered by taking an example in one direction. When a man suffers himself to be brought under by any one of these objects of his senses, and becomes a slave to it, we all know the effect on him: he is degraded, and becomes incapable of rising into spiritual freedom, and exertion, and dignity. It is manifest that they do produce an effect on the soul in this direction—that of evil. But is there none in the direction of good? The meanest thing that God hath created is fearfully and wonderfully made; adapted to its use with infinite and inconceivable skill. Is it likely, knowing the object which we know He had in Creation, that He should have lavished such skill on the inferior works of His hand, with no regard whatever to those for whom all this was made? Can a man therefore be safe in going through this world, making no use of the Creation of God, further than is required by his bodily wants and occupations? I have ever regarded it as one of the great arguments for imparting useful knowledge to all classes amongst us, that God evidently intended us to know and to admire and to behold Him in His works around us; and that therefore as long as we are not doing this, we are losing something which we might be gaining, and are defective for the higher purposes of our immortality. The beasts that perish stray over the plains and the mountain side, and look but on the grass whereon they browse: but man has special powers given to him to apprehend God's works, and to turn them into good for his undying spirit. It was for this that the Creator made the dreary abysses of space put on the lovely blue which arches over us, and caused the great light of the day to carry gladness to our sight, and decked the nightly heavens with glittering stars: for this that He so wonderfully turned aside the axis of our globe, and gave us the ever-varying round of seasons, so full of interest, and hope, and cheering prospect, and recurring toil: for this that He subjected to us the tribes of the earth, and air, and waters, for use, and for beauty, and for research: for this that He clad the earth in refreshing green, and enamelled her surface with a thousand blossoming gems, and gave us her manifold offspring, fruits, and herbs, and trees of the field. And the seas, and the mountains, and the plains, and the valleys, these He has made to be to us not mere accidents of the earth's surface, but never-failing wonders of refreshing beauty and grateful change: all for the teaching and nurturing and cheering of our spirits, whether by their own thoughts, or by their share in the invigoration of our bodies and renewal of our energies.

Let us approach somewhat closer this portion of our subject, and so draw our meditation towards its end. Let us boldly ask—what is the intent of these things which we see thus wonderfully and wisely made about us? What are we to think of Light, in which Creation lives and rejoices? What are we to believe respecting Life, that holy mystery which pervades this world of matter? What are we to say respecting the equally great mystery of food—the power granted to certain material substances to become portions of organized bodies, and supply their waste, and contribute to their growth? Are all these things mere happy contrivances of the Creator, to be admired for their wonderful skill and wisdom, but carrying no further lesson with them? Are they parts of *one* system, and is the Gospel of our Blessed Redeemer part of *another*? Do the processes of this world furnish no instruction to the Christian believer, and does the faith in Christ find no confirmation from the consideration of them?

Not so has our Redeemer Himself taught us; not so that beloved Apostle, who received the Holy Spirit of inspiration in the soaring rapture of the eagle's flight, and the undazzled steadiness of the eagle's gaze. Read the Gospel of St. John, and see there the natural philosophy of the faith: see there, not a number of ingenious similitudes to nature and her processes, but the true and ultimate science of Nature herself: learn thence, not that Christ is like light, is like life, is like food: but that light, life, and food all have their blessed qualities and their genial powers, *because they are* LIKE HIM. He is the true Light, He is the true Life, He is the Bread of Life, and the only real sustenance. Nature is but a stray spark, struck out from under the chariot-wheels of His path of Glory. Nature is but a shell cast up by the Ocean of His infinite love, in which the child-like listener may hear faintly and afar off the everlasting melodies of its unfathomable waters. The sun shines, because there is an Eternal Sun of Righteousness: the morning star burns on the kindling forehead of the East, because there is a blessed Day-star on high. The wind bloweth where it listeth, because there is a Divine Spirit moving over confusion and death and calling forth life: the tree puts forth her leaves and buds and blossoms and fruit, because there is a true Vine, with a multitude of fruit-bearing branches which no man can number: the wheat is laid in the ground as seed, and puts forth first the blade, then the ear, then the full corn in the ear, and is reaped, and gathered into barns, and threshed, and winnowed, and made into bread for man, not because of the necessities of nature, nor of man's fleshly body, but because there is a holy seed, even the word of God, capable of begetting man to a new life; because there is a growth in grace for the plants of our heavenly Father's planting, in which they ripen for His harvest, and shall be winnowed by His judgment, and laid up in His garner: because there is a blessed Bread of Life, which whoso eateth of shall live for ever. And so of a thousand processes of nature about us: they are because of, and they owe their creation to, eternal spiritual verities, of which the believer in Christ knows ever more and more, but of which he that believeth not, and the man of this world, knoweth nothing.

And what if the listener at the mouth of the shell sometimes hear the echo of other sounds than the gentle ripple sporting on the beach,—what if there be the striving of the winds of heaven on the sea, and the wailing of the rising gale, and the fierce conflict of the tempest at its height? Why are these heard in Nature? Why is there darkness, and blight, and dreariness, and disappointment, and decay, and death, but because all this has come first upon the spiritual world? There the sun has first been clouded, there the calm first disturbed; there the lurid form of evil appeared, before it blotted with its leaden mass the clear horizon of nature. When the Son of God passed into the shadow of His agony and the crisis of His dread conflict, the sun hid his face, and the earth was shaken: when the First-born of Creation was in anguish, the whole vast family was troubled, and the beauty of the heavens was saddened, and the foundations of the earth gave way.

Yes—this is the use of Nature, this is the end and aim of the Creation; to set forth God, to glorify Christ: to shadow forth the truth, as it is in the spirit of man, and as it is in God. Nature is not a ladder whereby to mount to Him: not a building of matter, on which we may climb up to heaven. There are no inferences from Creation which will lead men on to God. But nature is a ladder *let down from* God: a ladder at the top of which He stands as He has revealed Himself in Christ, and by the power of His Blessed Spirit. Revelation is the only key to Creation: the only solution of the ænigma of its use, as well as of its purpose and destiny. The Christian believer only can be the true naturalist; for he alone enters on the study of nature aright. He alone feels the ineffable majesty of that august temple of the Creator, and treads its aisles with the humility which leads to wisdom, and kneels at its altars with becoming devotion.

Its original purpose—its present purpose—these, as a Christian believer, I have thus endeavoured to enter into, writing for Christian believers, as a brother member of the Church, whose inheritance is this knowledge and this benefit.

One great inquiry yet remains: what will Creation be to us in the future? what shall be Nature's part, when Death shall have been swallowed up in victory?

III.

We stand at this point in our meditations. We have brought them to an end as regards this present state, and it is yet left for us to inquire concerning the use of Creation in the final glorious condition; whether it will have any use, and if any, what use, for the blessed in that other world. The former of these questions is very soon and very simply answered. The resurrection body will be created matter. However changed, however glorified, this will still be true of it. Our Lord's risen body was tangible by the disciples. It took into it the common food upon which we subsist. And as He challenged them to handle Him, and did eat and drink before them, with the set purpose of proving to them His identity, we are compelled to believe that both these,—the property of being handled, and the capacity of assimilating food,—were no visionary or assumed attributes of His glorified body, or else the proof would have been a mere delusion. That it could put off its liability to the observation of the senses, we know; that it needed not food for its subsistence, we may surely believe: but neither of these alters the above-mentioned facts. He was handled: and He did eat and drink. And as the firstfruits, so they that follow; not perhaps in all points, but certainly in all essential points. Our bodies will be risen, glorified, spiritual bodies: but they will still be bodies: created matter: and, as we before said, and I see not how we can escape inferring, living in a world of created matter.

Now, on the very threshold of this inquiry, one astonishing thing meets us, and it is this: that there should be those who call themselves Christians, and yet cast a doubt on the future resurrection of the body. I cannot see how a man who doubts this doctrine can be in any complete sense a Christian at all. If the dead rise not, then Christ is not risen; and if Christ is not risen, we are yet in our sins; our faith is vain, our preaching is also vain, and the gospel is a delusion. This is St. Paul's argument in that wonderful funeral chapter; and surely he who goes not with St. Paul in it, call himself what he will, is a mere unbeliever. And yet I fear there are many such: men who argue about that future state, that bodies will not be wanted there, and so on: neither knowing what they say, nor whereof they affirm. For if Christ has not saved man's body, He has not perfected that for which He came on earth; He has failed in that for which He died and rose again. It is indeed this doctrine, and not that of a future existence of the soul, which is the characteristic feature of Christianity.

I say no more on this point, but simply take it for granted, and proceed upon it as certain. We shall live for ever in the glorified body. Now what kind of circumstances will surround us in that new corporeal state? It is not easy, except for those who go to the Bible with the eye of their understanding shut, to mistake its testimony on this point. There are to be " new heavens and a new earth." "The whole creation," we are told, "groaneth and travaileth together in pain in this present state, waiting for the manifestation of the sons of God," *i.e.*, for the day when the sons of God shall be revealed and glorified, "because," the Apostle proceeds, " the Creation itself shall be delivered from the bondage of corruption into the liberty of the glory of the children of God."

Now these seem to be our facts to go upon. We need not seek further testimony: but may at once proceed to ask, what does this imply? As far as we are now capable of treating such a question, what are we to imagine respecting this new heaven and new earth,—this Creation freed from the bondage of corruption, and made partaker of the glory and freedom of the perfected children of God?

Now at this point we are met by the fact, that the question of the use of Creation in our future perfected state is, like some which we have considered in these meditations before, beset with considerable difficulties. Of these, some arise from the language of certain passages of Scripture, and others from the nature of the subject itself.

First, then, there is no denying that Holy Scripture seems in some places to speak as if this world, and all that is therein, were to bear no part at all in the employments and interests of those who shall inherit life eternal. The earth and the works therein are to be burnt up. All these things are to be dissolved; and considerations founded on that certainty are pressed upon us, as to affect our present practice. Again, we are told that the things seen are but for a time, whereas the things not seen endure for ever. And many passages of a similar tendency might be quoted. Are we, then, to understand these of a total annihilation and passing away of the fabric of material creation? Unexplained, it would seem as if we hardly could take them otherwise. But they are not left unexplained. Scripture also contains plain declarations, such as we have already quoted, not in figurative passages only, but in passages which cannot be taken otherwise than literally, that there must and will be a material creation, in the midst of which our future life will be spent. Not to mention at present the imagery which runs through the Prophets and the book of Revelation, which I venture to say can hardly have any sense assigned to it without such an assumption, the whole declarations of our Lord and His Apostles respecting the resurrection of the body absolutely require it, in order to fall into any connected and consistent meaning. Nay, we are not called upon to make any inferences of our own upon the point; for St. Paul himself distinctly gives us the testimony already cited, than which nothing can be plainer, that the world which we see about us shall not always be the prey of decay and disappointment, but shall itself be made partaker of the freedom and power of advance to perfection which shall result from the glorification of the triumphant Church. And it is clear, that one such plain declaration as this, which it is impossible to misunderstand, outweighs, by the very fact of its being the key to their true signification, any number of passages which seem to tend the other way. Their true sense must be made apparent by it, not its clear meaning explained away in order to bend it to them. If Creation is to be delivered from the fetters of decay, and wrong, and death, then must that burning up and dissolving, elsewhere spoken of, be the purifying and liberating process, not the exterminating and annihilating one.

So much may be laid down then as to the testimony of Scripture, that it is clear and precise concerning the future destiny of Creation. It is to partake of our blessedness; we are to have it about us, as we have the Creation about us here. Whether this is to take place on our globe, is for us perhaps an idle question, though we are naturally prone to ask it. There are in Scripture reasons for the supposition; and there are also reasons against it. And so too in the nature of things. This earth is full of the past: if it retained any of its distinctive features, would it not also, we may say, retain the traces of sin and sorrow? If it is not to retain those distinctive features, then it would matter little to us if it were to be locally and materially the same. At all events, whatever becomes of this lesser question, Scripture informs us that the Creation of God is not always to continue, as now, the prey of imperfection and blight and corruption; but that there is reserved for it, as well as for us, and for it as participating with us, a perfect and a glorious state.

I would not shrink from confessing (and this is that to which I alluded when I spoke of the difficulties of our subject) that the positive nature of those passages, especially that in 2 Peter iii., which seems to announce the destruction of nature, is, after all, somewhat perplexing. The idea that they describe a purifying process, though our only resource, does not seem an entirely satisfactory one. One other way indeed of explanation is open to us: that they may describe the destruction of *this* globe, and those other places may be spoken of some different ones. In this case, such words as those of St. Paul just now cited, " the Creation shall be delivered from the bondage of corruption," cannot mean what they almost must mean, that the same Creation which now suffers shall then be free from suffering.

And now let me pass on to the considerations arising out of the subject itself.

First of all then, there is this tendency in the affirmative direction. If we believe that Creation is but a part of Redemption, and with this belief we ask ourselves the question, Has Creation in this point of view. served its purpose? we surely must reply that it has not. The points of contact between man and the material world are very few. In those exercises and employments which most concern his eternal being, he secludes and insulates himself from it. Besides, it cannot be assumed to have served its purpose of bringing glory to God by the recognition of His wonderful works. In this present state, their mysteries are for the most part hidden from us. We know almost nothing about Creation. Its history indeed is told in Scripture in very general terms: but those terms themselves are mysterious; and when we compare them with the facts visible on the earth itself, we find that we have yet to learn how to understand many of them. And there can be no doubt that this will continue to be so to the end of time.

How little again do we know of the most interesting questions about Creation ? We examine, and we classify, and we speculate: but who can tell the processes, whereby the most ordinary phenomena in Nature take place? Who can satisfy us, why the leaf is green, and the flower constant to its own peculiar colour? Doubtless there might be an account given of the reason of all such facts; but at present they defy our analysis and baffle our research.

But will this always be so? Are we to imagine that God has created that most wonderful of His works, the mind of man, with faculties able to comprehend these inner mysteries of His creation, and then that such understanding is never to take place? Are we to believe that Nature is to be set before us, during our imperfect state here, as an enigma which we cannot solve, and that it will then, when we shall be endowed with superior faculties, be withdrawn from our observation? If this were so, then I must think that one of the great elements of the glorifying of God by His redeemed ones would be absent. So that on this ground, the nature of the case itself leads me to believe that a material

Creation will lie about us in that other state.

And if we inquire into the nature of our connection with and employment in that Creation, we must be guided to an answer, not by the very slight knowledge which we possess of the nature of the resurrection body, but by what seems to be the very first requisite of any idea at all which we can form of that future life, viz., that there must be continuity of being and interest in each one of us; that our life here and our life there should not be two distinct lives, but the continuation of one and the same life, however much that life may be ennobled, and exalted, and purified. Now what conclusions shall we draw from the application of this thought to our inquiry?

"At Thy right hand there is pleasure for evermore." What pleasure? Proceeding on the same course which we have just pointed out, we may say that surely this pleasure, for the majority of mankind, cannot be entirely disconnected from this present life here: will not be an entirely new beginning of a delight previously unknown, but the purification and ennobling of a delight already begun below. I know that this may seem strange to some :— that we have been accustomed to view that future state as a sort of great school of theology, in which we shall be always contemplating the great and difficult doctrines of the faith, and especially such of them as surpass and baffle us here. Doubtless in some cases this may be so; doubtless, in all cases, the mental vision will be so cleared and strengthened, that even those who were dullest on earth will be able to see and know more of the divine love and power, than could the ablest and deepest here: but this, I take it, is not the question: it is rather, whether the impressions and effects produced by what man has gone through here, will not be in the main the foundation of the exceeding blissfulness which he shall inherit there. And I venture to think that, if this is to be so, that a very large proportion of our impressions which we derive through the senses here will not be broken off and discontinued there, but will be carried forward in a more blessed and elevating form.

Let me without hesitation apply this to the consideration of our subject. And I will at once deal with a difficulty, which at first sight quite seems to baffle our powers. We cannot think of nature without decay. Decay is the very life of Nature, as now constituted. There is hardly one of her productions which does not, by its decay and corruption, furnish the essential material for supply and for subsistence. Remove decay, deliver nature from the bondage of corruption, and all things would be always the same: no pleasant succession, no interchange of grateful seasons. Bring all in nature to perfection, and stop all at that point,—and, however beautiful, the face of the new earth would seem to be but as a picture, and that an incongruous one.

This then it would appear cannot be meant by deliverance from the bondage of corruption. The words must somehow bear another and a worthier sense. It cannot be that the world, in her change into a fit habitation for the blessed for ever, should lose all that beauty and that glory which carried gladness to our hearts before. Some things indeed belonging to the present state we can hardly admit in our thoughts into that other: the desolating storm, the withering blight, the nipping frost, the unfruitful season,—these, and the like of these, cannot be where all is free to expand, and where the meanest child of nature will not fail to reach its best and highest degree. And we may well conceive also, that certain combinations of circumstances, to which we owe much of our enjoyment of nature here, will hardly be found there. The first outbreak of spring makes the heart leap within us, chiefly perhaps because of the winter, which has so long bound up vegetation with his icy fetters: when the woods put on their fresh green, and the earth on which we tread becomes radiant with flowers, it is above all things the contrast which gives zest and delight. But we can hardly imagine that there will be winter there; or that bareness and dreariness will ever characterize the hills and vales of the new earth. And if we pursue the train of thought thus suggested, we may perhaps arrive at some account of how this may well be. Here, in our weak and ever changing state of thought and feeling, contrast is always necessary to add piquancy to our interest. There, where satisfied calm shall have taken the place of restless craving for change, contrast will no longer be wanted. To our ears now, perpetual spring sounds as if it would soon pall upon us: and even if there could be a happy mixture of the three propitious seasons, and the earth could at one and the same time be budding into leaf, and opening the flower, and ripening the fruit, it might be a question whether our senses would not soon weary of the continual strain on them, and yearn for some entire rest, some fallow time like winter, when they might repose from excitement.

But there, it may well not be so. Weariness will no longer exist: good enjoyed will lead on to good desired: the eye will not want respite from seeing, nor the ear from hearing, nor the brain from searching and gaining conclusions. So that it may well be, that there shall be no decay there, and yet no feeling of dulness; no desire for change, where the thoughts and interests themselves will be always changing, because always advancing from one height of blessedness to another.

And if a further consideration is wanted to

convince us, that there may be the highest bliss in the enjoyment and contemplation of God's works, without the elements of decay and renewal, we may think of what will be our own state in that other life, and derive from that a strong argument as to the condition of the blessed world itself of which we shall form a part. We are told by our Lord, that we shall be like the holy angels; ourselves without death and decay, and therefore without the necessity of renewal. Doubtless there will be beauty there, far surpassing the fairest dream here; there will be majesty there, compared to which all the splendour of man here is but contemptible: but there will be no fluctuation—no oscillating backwards and forwards into degrees of greater or less: either all will be always the same, or the only progress will be advance.

And as man himself will be, so in all likelihood will also be the world in which man will be found. Here, decay and change are the very conditions of beauty and majesty. The loveliness of infancy, the gaiety of childhood, the strength and comeliness of youth, the force of manhood, the veneration claimed for age, the sympathies called forth by feebleness, the solemn lessons bequeathed us by death, — all these are but circumstances attendant on so many onward steps in a course which reaches its height and then declines. But there, all these, or as many of them as are consistent with a blissful state of perfection, will be fixed at their height and their best, and there will for ever continue to flourish, filled with loveliness and purity, according to the measure of each, by Him, the great author and source of all that is lovely and pure. Each, we may well conceive, will have its place and its work, and in that place and work will be an element in the multitudinous blessedness of the whole. And even so will it be with Creation itself. Of whatever members and details Creation may then consist, whether of the same that we see here, or more, or less, each will be advanced to its highest point of perfection, each will have attained all its possible beauty and majesty, and at this point will remain for ever. As the blessed contemplate the wonderful works of God, new wonders, fresh points of interest, will continually occur: more praise will be rendered to Him, more true pleasure will accrue to His redeemed ones, throughout the countless ages of eternity.

And if it be asked, how is this to be, seeing that all Creation has inherited man's sin, seeing that the ground is cursed for his sake, and nature suffers because the lord of nature was disobedient?—we may fearlessly reply, it will take place, this deliverance from the bondage of corruption and of sin, owing to the Death and Resurrection of the Lord. Having made peace by the blood of His cross, by Him it pleased the Father to reconcile all things to Himself, all things in heaven and earth. And in that vision of St. Peter, when he was instructed not to call that unclean which God had cleansed, this was distinctly set forth to him: this bringing of all things created into a state of reconcilement with God, and fitting use for man, by the great sacrifice of the Death of the Son of God. So that I believe we may surely expect, and I do myself confidently look for, this renewed and glorious condition of God's material Creation in the next happy state. I believe nature has not been, as the loose belief of many would suppose it to have been, a great mistake on the part of the Creator— a gigantic failure—an imperfect mould, to be cast aside one day as though it had never been; but I hold firmly that for even material nature there is a good time coming, when the desert shall rejoice and blossom as the rose:—that God's wonderful works, here so much abused, so little understood, will there, in all their highest forms of beauty and proportion, be the everlasting study and admiration of the blessed. Not, it is true, before, still less to the exclusion of, His still more wonderful work of Redemption, but as contributing to it, and indeed themselves forming part of it.

And this leads us to the same point where we brought to a close our other meditations: that it is for the sake of Christ, and of Christ's work of love, and of Christ's redeemed ones, that all things are and were created. For this will be then most clearly shown and most fully carried out, when not only the Church, but material Nature also, has reached its highest aim and end: when no decay mars the one, as no sin the other: when the wonders of the created universe are read, not as now, with failing eyes and doubting hearts, but with the purified and unerring vision of the sons of God in glory; when there will be no peril of science invading faith, because faith and knowledge will be one: when none can go astray, because He who made and who redeemed all things will be Himself our teacher, and will lead us beside the fountains of living waters; when great acquirements will no longer mar perfect holiness, because He who sanctifieth the elect people of God will dwell in us, in full measure, for ever.

ON PROVIDENCE.

I.

DIFFICULTIES OF THE MAIN SUBJECT.

WE speak and we write evermore of GOD'S PROVIDENCE. We regard Him as ruling over the world, and shaping all things after the counsel of His own will. This is our belief.

But at the same time, we speak and we write evermore also of *man* as the moving cause of events and results in this world. If we do, or abstain from doing, this or that, we regard certain consequences as sure to follow. And in common life, we ordinarily act as if there were no power superior to ourselves, to interfere with the course and the products of human actions. This is our practice.

Now this belief on the one hand, and this practice on the other, are common to all orders and kinds of men in our Christian land: to the most devoutly religious, as well as to those whose religion sits most loosely upon them. We ordinarily speak and write, in our more serious moods, as if God were down on earth, walking among us, arranging and ordering everything: we ordinarily speak, write, and act, in the common affairs of life, I will not say as if there were no God, but certainly as if He were at a distance from us, and did not meddle in human affairs.

The occurrence of such a diversity between men at one time and the same men at another, a diversity so universally found prevailing, and taken so much as a matter of course, naturally sets one thinking as to whether any reasonable account can be given of it, or whether it is quite unreasonable and blameable. And it is plain that this train of thought, if followed out, will take us over some considerable space, and cost us no little trouble. We shall find ourselves compelled to trace up some of those ideas, which we usually accept without inquiry, even to their very sources: and to give an account of some ways of speech and habits of action, which seem to us almost as instincts, born with us, and always found in us.

Notwithstanding, it does appear to me important that such an inquiry should be undertaken. We live in days when many and many a talent is folded round and round with napkins, and buried deep in the earth: when many holy words, which ought to be full of stirring significance, have been sounding so long in the air, that they have become but as tinkling noises: when, to take another figure, every portion of our spiritual armour wants separately looking up, and burnishing, and oiling afresh, if it is ever to be used to any purpose.

Let us then meditate awhile on God's Providence: on our ideas of it, as connected with the actions of men, and with our own course in life. And may His Spirit guide us aright.

It seems first requisite that we should give some account of our idea of God Himself, with reference to our main subject. We are apt to take for granted that all is clear about the infinite power and capacity of God, without considering what a strange and wonderful thing it is that we are believing. The common, and the true idea of God is, that He knows and orders all things. But let us follow this out in our thoughts. All that we can conceive about a mind, and its knowledge, is derived from what we observe about our own minds, and the minds of other men. Now what is your knowledge, and what is mine? The merest imperfect fragment of what is to be known about even that little which falls under our own observation. When we take into account, on the one hand, our ignorance, our forgetfulness, our misapprehensions,—and on the other, the number of things which we might know, but which escape us, and the number which, to make our knowledge worth anything, we ought to know, but cannot attain to, and then reflect, that of the sons of men, he who knows most is equally liable to these imperfections with him who knows least,—truly we must see that every thing we can conceive about an all-extensive and a perfect knowledge must be delusive indeed, and short of any even the least adequate idea. God, we believe, knows all things. Now, let us try to realize such a kind of knowledge even within small limits. Suppose, to begin with very little, that any of us could retain in his mind, perfectly, and without fail, everything that had come under his observation for a whole month, or week, or day. What an amazing mass of knowledge it would be! All the shifting thoughts that flitted through the mind; all the insignificant objects that passed before the eye; all the looks, and words, and doings of his fellow-men. And yet this is perfection only in one department of knowledge,—only in the power of retaining in the memory: and even this would be enough to weigh down and overbear the powers of any human mind. In the presence of such a supposition, we congratulate ourselves on our power of forgetting, and look on it as one of the best safeguards of our health and peace of mind. Yet in thinking of God, we are imagining to ourselves a Being in whose knowledge are absolutely abiding all things that ever were in this world, and, for aught we can tell, in myriads of worlds besides.

But again, let us vary our supposition, and try to conceive what it would be, if any one of us knew everything present around him. What would it be, for instance, if I knew all that was passing in that limited space which is before my eyes at this moment? Only try to realize such a thought, and it utterly baffles our conception. Take even one minutest portion of that space: it is filled with air, whose composition it surpasses human science thoroughly to describe and account for; that portion of atmosphere is peopled perhaps with life so minute as to escape the subtlest instruments by which our eyes are assisted; or it is occupied by solid material, wood or stone, whose very texture is a mystery, in the one case of the special organized vegetable growth, in the other of the deposition of strata older than the system of nature under which we live. Or, for our supposition must extend even to this in order to be complete, the portion of space on which we look may contain that greatest of all mysteries for man to behold, the countenance of man : and then we must be able to read every one of its expressions, and to declare all the thoughts of which they are the signs. It seems to me, that for any one man thoroughly and entirely to know the recesses of the mind of another, would be a weight of knowledge and anxiety sufficient to drive reason from its seat, and destroy the power of knowledge altogether. And yet when we conceive of God, we imagine a Being who knows absolutely all things that are: who penetrates every mystery, and before whom no secrets are hid: who knows the thoughts of all hearts: whose field of view is not one small portion of space, but the whole universe. If it would be more than man could bear, to be admitted into the recesses of another mind besides his own, what would it be, to hold at once in knowledge the hidden thoughts of a whole family—a whole city—a whole nation—all mankind—the inhabitants, it may be, of millions of worlds? Yet this, and no less than this, must be true of God. No less, but much more than this: for to all this we must add the absolute knowledge of all things to come; the entire guidance and ordering of all things, from the greatest down to the most minute, in every place and at every time.

Now I say these things about the knowledge of God, that I may make it appear, not how vast it is, far passing in comprehension anything of which we can form an idea (for this is not my present object), but that it is something, in its very kind and nature, different from that which we call knowledge. . It is absolute and all-including. Not only all existing things, but also all sources and reasons of things, and all the issues and ends of things, are taken in by it. And again, it is not knowledge, as ours is, of that which is outside, and independent of Himself. Whatever God knows, He also is Himself concerned with, and has the absolute disposal of. He is the centre of life, and of power; in Him all things live, and move, and have their being.

Now it must be evident, if we give thought to the matter, that we cannot expect to comprehend the sort of interference which knowledge like this exercises in human affairs. The whole subject is too vast for our grasp. We have no faculties with which to approach its consideration. It is totally unlike any case in our own matters, which one might at first sight be disposed to compare with it. Let us take one, and we shall see this. If a man claims what we call previous knowledge of the way in which a course of events will turn out, it can only be from long exercise of his observation on similar occurrences; and this is but a conjecture after all, more or less to be relied on, according to the amount of his experience, and the accurate exercise of his judgment. And after all, he is obliged to allow for all sorts of unlooked-for contingencies, which may throw out his calculation. In fact, such a claim, on such grounds, does not properly belong to man at all; still less does any control over those who act in any course of events. We may be, in some sense, controlled by other men: yet it is not because we are compelled to be obedient to their will, but, however far compulsion may seem to extend, it is, really and ultimately, because we choose to be; because we see the necessity for so being obedient. Even the man whose power of action is most completely taken from him by the will of another,—even the prisoner in the dungeon, may die when his tyrant would have him live: even the victim on the scaffold, over

ON PROVIDENCE.

whom outward circumstances seem all-powerful, so that he must die, may rise in will and in word above them. It is plain that we cannot compare for a moment such knowledge, or such power, with that all-embracing sovereignty of God, concerning which we are now treating. And what is the inference from that which has been said? Clearly, it seems to me, this: that we have no right to think of God's foreknowledge, and control of our ways and course of life, as we would think of the same in a fellow-creature; because the two are totally different in the most essential points. God's foreknowledge and control embraces all things at once. Every law which affects His creatures, and every capacity of choice and action on the part of any of His creatures, is included in that, His foreknowledge and control, just as completely as the results of those laws and capacities. Our free will is just as much His appointment, as anything else which belongs to us: as our power, for instance, of breathing or walking.

He knows beforehand how we shall exert it: but that foreknowledge of His does not fetter its exertion. We know that we do exert it hour by hour; we feel that courses of action or inaction lie open to our choice. Nothing can ever rob us of this conviction. If we are constrained to do this, or not to do that, it is not, we know it is not, a power above us which forces us, but it is the guidance of our own judgment, the verdict of our own deliberation, the sense of our own interest, the appreciation of circumstances known and taken into account by ourselves: God being the appointer of those circumstances, and the appointer also of our being set to choose among them. It has ever seemed to me one of the most astonishing things, that any thinking persons should be found, who deny the free will of man. For of all facts open and undeniable, this appears to me the most conspicuous, and the least able to be controverted. And hence it is that, as I said in the beginning, we ever speak and act, in ordinary life, on the full assumption of the exercise of this free will. All human affairs proceed on it. Without it, there would be no moral responsibility at all. No man would be accountable in the slightest degree for acts or words which were totally independent of his own choice. Without freedom of the human will, our teaching would be vain, and our faith would be vain also. What are the words of Scripture exhortation? "Behold I set before you this day life and death: therefore choose life, that it may be well with thee." Did not the Redeemer stand and invite all weary and heavy-laden to come to Him? Did He not, on the other hand, charge the Jews, as a fault, that they were not willing to come unto Him that they might have life? And when St. Paul used the strongest term he could use, and said, "The love of Christ constraineth us," did He not make this very constraint the result of our own deliberate judgment, and say, "The love of Christ constraineth us, because we thus judge, that if one died for all, then all died?" And we might go further, and say, If man were not free to be affected this or that way by considerations presented to him, why has the Spirit of God pleaded all these ages with sinful men? Why all this exhibition of God's love in order to move our love? We love Him, not because He compels us to love Him, not because we cannot help it, which would take all the reality out of love, but because He first loved us. He draws us with the cords of a man, His heart to our heart, for our good, and for His glory in our good. And the same thing which is true in our determinations about the most solemn things, is true also in all the ordinary matters of life. We act, and we are expected to act, as being free to choose our course of action. Hence comes, and hence properly and legitimately comes, that which we mentioned in the beginning, the universal habit of men, religious as well as irreligious, of going on in life, and speaking and acting from day to day, as possessing this freedom, and, within certain limits, guiding themselves by it. If they did not, they would not be fit for the world's business, or the world's duties: they would in fact cease to be rational beings at all.

But we must not leave the matter here. We have, I think, to the minds of reasonable men, made clear one point: that, our own free will being a plain fact, and as matter of fact not hindered from moment to moment by special interference from above, we are meant to act as being free, and to be invested with a responsibility which depends on that freedom.

And we have further shown, I trust, that the undeniable foreknowledge and sovereignty of God, being a matter so far passing our comprehension, and so far removed from anything which we know of in practical life, cannot be, and ought not to be, brought in as a disturbing element in our ordinary reasonings and conclusions on matters presented to us in life.

I said, we must not stop here. For, if we did, there might appear to be some danger of our being understood to mean, that we ought to go our way in life without thinking of God, or acknowledging His guiding and superintending hand. And this would be the very contrary of that which we really do intend: having undertaken the consideration of this matter, in order that, if it may be, we may shew how the recognition of God should be our constant safeguard and guide in life, and our greatest comfort in all that befalls us. "Man's goings," says the scripture, "are of the Lord: how then can he understand his own way?" (Prov. xx. 24.) These words contain the whole matter. God's foreknowledge, God's superintending Providence, enwraps us all round. It is like the space through which our globe revolves: like the air which we breathe as we move about on it. It is a necessary condition of our living, and moving, and having our being. As we cannot think of material objects without space being presupposed for them to be situated in—as we cannot think of a succession of events without presupposing time for them to happen in, so neither can we conceive of a world at all, or of ourselves as existing in that world, without presupposing the foreknowledge and sovereignty of God, who created and upholds it. Man's goings are of the Lord. If this be not so, God is not the King of all: God is not God. This is a fact incontrovertible, and not to be shaken: necessary from our very idea of a God at all. And now comes the inference: "Man's goings are of the Lord: how then can he understand his own way?" How can we expect to be able to bring down the surpassing vastness of God's foreknowledge and power, and to fit it on to the petty details of our individual lives? We cannot do it: we shall err grievously, if we attempt to do it. What is the lesson then, —the lesson which good sense and Scripture alike teach us? Why this;—not to attempt it: to recognise to the full *both* the great facts,— God's sovereignty, and man's free will,—and to go no further. We can see these two clearly.

Their lines are plainly marked, running on side by side through our lives, and through the lifetime of our world. But to trace them up into one, the human eye fails. Bring them ever so near, by reasoning or by illustration, yet the point where they join is lost in the light inaccessible, which no man hath seen nor can see. Many have tried to gaze on it; many are trying now:—but the result is ever the same; the presumptuous eye is dazzled, the overbold inquirer strays into error, and the mystery remains where it was. Let us rather keep our thoughts intent on the work in life which God our Father hath given us to do; it will require all our energy to carry it on, and all our penetration to discern what His will is in it respecting us. In it, apportioned by His good Providence who has created both the shoulder and the burden, will be found our most healthy and our wisest employ; there shall we meet with Him who can give us strength, and whose presence alone can cheer the journey through life. We cannot understand our own way, it is true; but for this very reason, that our goings are of Him. He is about our path, and about our bed, and spieth out all our ways. He has taken care that our whole lives should be full of Him, and of the thought of Him. His blessed Son has lived our life, has felt our sorrow, has died our death. Wherever we are in the world, the tracks of His footsteps are visible before us. God's knowledge may be too vast for us to imagine: His power and sovereignty may be elements too weighty to enter into our daily thought of the details of our lives; but Jesus our Lord hath manifested Him to us, and in our Redeemer's presence we can look on God and live. The evident freedom of our will then is no excuse for forgetting God. They who acknowledge not Him in their goings, use not that freedom aright. Rather let us adore the mystery of His loving-kindness, who has so wonderfully made us that, while we are in His hands as clay in those of the potter, He has yet left each of us in the free use of those powers and faculties which He has given us, who, in the great conflict between good and evil, has overcome our evil with His good; being the Father of lights, from whom is every good and perfect gift,— ever waiting to be gracious to us,—ever offering us the help of His free Spirit. Rather let us strive, each in his place, to seek after Him, and feel His hand leading us; and thus, though we may not understand our own way in life, we shall be guided on by Him who doeth all things well, from faith, to the sight of Him: from a limited and imperfect existence, to the liberty of the glory of the sons of God.

II.

GOD'S GUIDANCE OF US FOR GOOD.

IN our last meditation on the Providence of God, we endeavoured to shew that His foreknowledge and power were matters so infinitely surpassing our comprehension, that while we are certain that all our ways are ordered by Him, we cannot understand our own path, nor the manner in which His will foreordains it; that consequently we cannot, and in fact no man does, take into account, in the details of our daily life, that foreknowledge and power as a disturbing element. It envelopes us, and is all about us; but, at the same time, our will is free to choose and to refuse courses of action proposed to us; and if it were not, we should no longer be accountable beings.

We will now look at the same great subject from another side. We will inquire respecting the tender and constant care with which God, ever present and ever watchful, upholds and provides for us. If it be true, that we have no right to regard Him, in ordinary cases, as interfering with the exercise of our own free will in choosing between courses of action, are we justified in assuming that His providence watches over us for good, and guides our feet into the way of peace? In other words, is there, I will not say any inconsistency, but any blameable inconsistency, any inconsistency that we can help, in refusing to think of God as an obstacle to our freedom of action, and yet claiming to think of Him as the constant witness of all that we do, and our never-wearied Benefactor and Upholder?

The answer to this question will somewhat depend on some things which were said in our last meditation. The reason why we cannot regard God as interfering with the exercise of our own free will is, that his foreknowledge and power are too vast for our comprehension, are matters which we cannot by any possibility bring down and apply to the details of our ordinary life without the danger of continually going wrong. Man's goings are of the Lord: and therefore he cannot understand his own way. On the other hand, we know and are sure, that we have the free choice between courses of action. And it is not for us to misinterpret, and to mar the healthy conditions of, a portion of our being, whose wholesome exercise, in accordance with the divine will, is our very secret of moral happiness, by mixing it up with another high and mysterious matter which we cannot comprehend. This was our argument. How does it apply here?

God is to us the author of all that is good. Whenever comfort comes, whenever preservation comes, whenever body or soul is benefited, the gift is of Him, and not of man, nor of ourselves, in the first degree. Thus much is perfectly clear. In a given case, perhaps, we chose the good and refused the evil. But it was He who put it into our hearts to choose the good; it was He who gave us strength, when we had chosen it, to follow up our inclination and resolve; it was He who moved obstacles out of our way; it was He who turned even our evil into His good, and shaped and moulded men and events so that we might attain unto that good. And all this was not by forcing us into accord with Him and His will, but by gentle persuasion, and by putting opportunities in our way, and by the pleadings of His blessed indwelling Spirit. The bad man may refuse to hear God, and go his way, and act independently; the good man may partially listen to Him, and may sometimes prefer his own inclination to the prompting of the Spirit for His good; but the great truth remains the same: that it is God who is striving for the welfare, and providing for the necessity, and upholding the life, temporal and spiritual, of us all. If there be an inconsistency here, it is at least one bound up with our very first conditions of thought and feeling. It is at least one which we, in our present imperfect state, cannot help, and are even bound to submit to. Where we cannot see God's way clear, nor understand how He shapes our course, we proceed on the known fact of our own free will, and regard ourselves as responsible, and in some measure as the pilots of our own way; but where we can see Him, and all is clear, we love to acknowledge His hand and to praise

His goodness, and to trace His beneficent interference in warding off evil, and in procuring us good. There is, in fact, no more inconsistency here than in the seaman, who, while the sky is clear and the sun and stars visible, takes his observations direct from them, and steers accordingly; but when they become overcast, has recourse to his books and his instruments, and shapes his course as he best may. The one guidance may be surer than the other; but both are in compliance with the laws of the same world, and both are with a view to the same end. And if it be most true, that God is about us when we do not see Him, and girds us when we know Him not, the very acknowledgment of this fact ought to show us, that it is in vain for us to attempt to recognise all the ways by which He leads us, but that we must be content to appear very often to be left to ourselves; while at the same time we must none the less for this be tracing Him where we can, and attributing to Him at least all those portions of our course which seem to bear traces of His good and merciful guidance.

Let us now strengthen this position by the direct testimony of Holy Scripture. I said before, that it is the practice of the word of God, in the case of great truths which may seem to our minds to be inconsistent with each other, not, as we do, to trim and compromise between them, but to state both sides broadly and plainly, and leave us to infer that the putting both together surpasses our powers. In no case is this more evident, than in the statements of Scripture respecting God's Providence and man's free will. The statement of the latter truth engaged us in our former meditation. We quoted words which offered to man the choice of life and death, and we might have quoted questions which imply that the death of the sinner was his own act, and not that of God. But the assertions respecting God's watchful Providence, and universal foreknowledge, and unresisted sovereignty, are as plain and undoubted. Take that of our Lord, where He says that two sparrows are sold for a farthing, and yet that, without the knowledge of God, and His permission, not one of these shall perish; —and goes on to say, that the very hairs of our heads are all numbered: meaning, that nothing befalls us, unknown to, unwatched by, unpermitted by, our heavenly Father. Take any portion of Holy Scripture, either history or prophecy, or the confessions of any of the servants of God with regard to their personal life and experience,—and it is ever the same. God is seen everywhere. He girds them to war. He blesses them with peace. He brought them from the womb, and cared for them when they hanged yet on their mothers' breasts. From youth up until now;—even to hoar hairs and the day of death,—He carries them. They are safe under the shadow of His wings, and His ministering messengers bear them up in their hands, lest at any time they should dash their foot against a stone. Such has ever been the expressed belief, such have been the motives for courage and confidence and resignation, of all the servants of God: from the first days of the dawning promise, until the full light of the Sun of Righteousness arose upon the Church. Such was the feeling of Moses, and of Joshua, and of David, and of Elijah, and of Hezekiah, and of Nehemiah, and of the prophets: such was the conviction of St. Paul, and of St. Peter, and of all the holy men who wrought and suffered for Christ. And such, above all, was ever the mind and the confession of Him who is our pattern as well as our propitiation. The Lord Jesus, in His course on earth,—yea, more, in His course through glory to perfection in heaven,—ever regarded Himself as in the watchful care of the Father, sent upon earth to do His will, not alone, even in the hour of dark desertion and bitter suffering, because the Father was with Him. There can be no doubt, that the tendency of all Scripture teaching and example, as well as of its direct command, is to induce us to see God in all our ways, and acknowledge Him in all our paths,—that it is to lead us to do this, infinitely more than we are disposed to do it. Our tendency is to forget God, and to look too much to ourselves and to men around us; but the man who reads his Bible will evermore find this tendency counteracted by the assertion of God's presence, and God's working, and God's crossing his path at every turn.

And let us come, as usual in these meditations, from the more general consideration of our state as believers in God, to that of our more particular condition as believers in the Son of God. If, in the former capacity, we are bound by God's word to see Him ever about us, surely in the latter we are much more bound. For consider what He has done to assert more strongly His presence with us, and His care over us. He has entered into our nature; and become, not merely what He was to the ancient Church, a covenant God, but, according to His promise, God manifest in our flesh: dwelling and abiding among us as one of ourselves. The Son of God is no God at a distance, removed from our yearnings and our sympathies. Are we tempted? He has been tempted in like manner. Are we in pain? He has suffered likewise. Are we deserted, in bereavement, and in sorrow? So was He: it was the very form which He took on Him and the very character by which He was pleased to be known. Of old, it was obvious to the mind of God's servants to see Him about them in prosperity; but difficult to trace Him in adversity. All they could attain to was a general confidence that He would provide well, and a resolve to leave all to Him. "Cast thy burden upon the Lord, and He shall sustain thee." "I have been young and now am old, and yet never saw I the righteous forsaken, nor his seed begging their bread." Even to us now, such pious sayings are most touching, and full of comfort; but it is mainly by the light shed on them since the Man of Sorrows has gone up into His glory.

Now, it is not a vague confidence that all things will be well which upholds us: it is no mere result of a life-long experience that all will be well with the righteous. Ours is a far higher and a far more blessed faith and persuasion. Suffering and sorrow, contradiction and desertion, persecution and death, these were the appointed and the chosen paths of Him who loved us, and washed us from our sins in His blood. Through these dark and dreary valleys sparkles the track of those footsteps which are now lost in the light unapproachable. Blessed are they who follow Him anywhere: twice blessed they who are made partakers of His sufferings: most blessed of all, they who drink deepest of that cup, round which is inscribed in letters of light, " Not my will, but thine be done." We suffer, we mourn, with no mere vague persuasion that all will be well: with no mere regard to the dealings of a God at a distance, moving and working in the history of those we have known: such thoughts may tend to uphold our weakness, may be sometimes the highest we can reach : but O they are not our birthright, they are not the extent of our high privilege. We have rights in Christ extending far beyond these. We are the sheep of Christ following their Shepherd: none can pluck us out of His hand: if we be found in the path in which He went before, not mere resignation, but triumph and holy joy should be our mind.

Such thoughts as these lead me to conclude with one or two remarks, both respecting the blessedness of the Christian who thus sees God about his path, and respecting the wise and sober limits within which such blessedness is found.

There is no surer way to real happiness, than a constant sense of God's upholding and providing care. For one who earnestly believes that which is said of Him in Scripture and the offices of the Church, life may indeed be, as it is to other men, full of difficulty, and of dark places; but there hath arisen a light in his darkness. There can be no gloom in his path, though there

ON PROVIDENCE. 163

may be shade. There can be no distressing doubt, though there may be uncertainty. There can be no despair, though there may be necessity for entire resignation into his Father's hand. He need not be afraid of any evil tidings, for his heart standeth fast, trusting in the Lord. He may be left alone, but his Father is with him. None may uphold him in his path of chosen duty, but the witness of the Spirit is more to him than the applause of the multitude. Listen to the language of such an one in old time: "The Lord is my Shepherd; I shall not want. He maketh me to lie down in green pastures: He leadeth me beside the still waters. He restoreth my soul: He leadeth me in the paths of righteousness for His name's sake. Yea, though I walk through the valley of the shadow of death, I will not fear: for thou art with me; thy rod and thy staff they comfort me. Surely goodness and mercy shall follow me all the days of my life: and I will dwell in the house of the Lord for ever."

Words like these bring us to our last consideration, and lead us to say, that the true enjoyment of this abiding feeling of God's gracious and loving guidance is to be gained, not by an unbridled fancy, nor by a superstitious magnifying of ordinary circumstances into extraordinary, but by the combined exercise of earnest piety with sound discretion. On the one hand, let us never think that we ourselves alone are the objects of God's care; on the other hand, let us never fail to acknowledge that care keeping watch over us. The best rule for a sober judgment in this matter will be derived from the considerations which have been already before us in these meditations. No sober-minded Christian will ever see God acting as fettering or hindering his way, but will choose according to his heavenly Father's will, in a free and loyal spirit. Again, no wise man will trouble himself with dispensations of God's Providence which we cannot possibly understand. Such thoughts frequently perplex and distress men beyond measure, but surely not those men who give sober consideration to the subject. What are called special providences may be difficult to recognise, and dangerous to press on the mind as such: but in fact they are all around us, and universal. The ship goes its way with its freight and its passengers, and is overwhelmed in the storm. He who hastened to set sail in her, and was too late, is on all hands acknowledged to have been the subject of God's providential and special care. But are we to say that no such special providence kept watch over those who perished in her? God forbid. Every one of them was just as much in the mind of our heavenly Father as he who was saved. His course was continued, theirs was brought to an end: but the same loving-kindness was over both, and the same infinite wisdom shewn in the lot apportioned to each. The man in health and vigour praises God for the lengthened time of his service, and the continued power of active good: are we to suppose on this account that the poor invalid, whose life is confined to the walls of his chamber, is forgotten by God? No indeed; he may praise Him just as much and as heartily for his hour of calm slumber, for his interval of rest from pain, and sweet meditation. The aged servant of God looks back on a long career, and glorifies Him for the mercies of years: but his mercies to the youth or the maiden cut down in the flower of life are just as great in their kind, just as worthy of praise. Let each trace God about his own path: there he may see in abundance the power of the Father, the love and sympathy of the Son, the inner pleading and witness of the Spirit. The course of others, and some parts of his own, may be dark and perplexing to him; concerning these let him not be troubled. Enough is revealed, enough is quite clear, for continual thanks and praise: enough to prompt ever-growing trust and ever-increased resignation.

Let us live closer and closer to Him; ever

feeling for His hand to guide,—ever looking for His light on our path: and then we shall be safe in life, safe in death, and blessed for ever.

III.

TESTIMONY FROM THE COURSE OF THE WORLD.

In the course of meditating on the Providence of God, our attention is naturally drawn to the evidence furnished by the moral state of things around us. On which side does this tell? Does it appear, when we take it into account, as if things drifted onward by blind chance? does it seem as if man unassisted shaped his own course? or does it seem as if an unseen hand were guiding? To employ our time in answering this question, may seem like taking superfluous trouble, seeing that it is abundantly answered for us in Holy Scripture, and to entertain any doubt on it would be so far to set aside the great verities of our Christian faith. Yet it is profitable sometimes (and this is especially the case in days like our own, when the foundations of the faith are assailed) to derive confirmation for our faith, by looking at matters around us, just as any mere observer must look at them: and to endeavour to lift up the unbelieving or the doubting to us, by seeming for a while to come down to their level, and to speak as they do.

Well then, let us begin with a general survey of the state of things around us with regard to good and evil. It is, I suppose, pretty plain to all, that our natural tendency, if left entirely to ourselves, is to evil. One need but look at the state of the heathen nations: one need but observe the course of any person growing up without educational training, to be convinced of this. And I do not know that any reasonable person seriously questions it. We sometimes hear rash expressions of a contrary opinion thrown out, but it is generally by men of a peculiar stamp, fond of maintaining singular views: and I have generally observed, that they who thus speak, do nevertheless in their actions, and in the business of life, just as much

ON PROVIDENCE. 169

take for granted a general tendency to evil as the rest of mankind. Well then, this being so,—man being generally prone to evil,—when we look about over the world and the face of society, one question at once meets us: How is it that the world is not worse than it is? Take the state of the very lowest and the most depraved among the heathen tribes,—and why is not that the state of us all? Why has not every nation, through its successive generations, gravitated constantly downward? To this question there may be two answers. The downward tendency must have been checked either by some influence within man, arising from himself, or by some influence without him, arising from some one not himself. Let us consider each of these in turn. If the salutary influence is to be attributable to upward and nobler instincts in man, how is it that these have acted in some cases, and have been altogether dormant in others? It may be said, that this has been according as they have met with favourable or unfavourable circumstances of situation or climate. But it is easily answered, that this is remarkably otherwise. The fairest portions of the earth have sometimes witnessed the most appalling degradation of our race, as is now the case in many places under the tropical climates: while at the same time some of those fairest portions have seen the most remarkable development of the moral conscience and of the intellectual power of man; as for instance the Land of Promise of old, and the lovely shores and valleys of ancient Greece. And on the other hand, the hardest and most ungenial climates have not prevented human progress to good, as neither can they be said to have always promoted it. We have examples of some of the best of nations struggling with the disadvantages of soil and sky, and some of the worst succumbing under them. It would seem as if we were especially cautioned by facts, not to fall into the mistake of imagining that man is made or unmade by outward circumstances.

For the very same situations and climates have been the scenes, at different times, of the most widely various phenomena in the history of mankind. The land where all Israel once dwelt peaceably under David and Solomon is now well-nigh desolate, and the traveller goes in peril of the plundering Arab. This country of ours, now teeming with inhabitants peaceful and loyal, was once the war-ground of savages; and where our churches now rise, human sacrifices were offered. If we look again at mere situation, the same advantages which at one time may seem to have made a nation of busy and successful traders, have at another reared a nest of pirates and marauders.

Nor again can it be said that influences for good have been implanted in some races of men, while others have been without them. Vast as the difference really is between the races of men as we now find them, such a view seems to me wholly to misrepresent it. It is one not so much of good and evil, as of comparative power for both. The superior race is not superior in good alone, but in evil also. Its advances in true civilization and social purity are ever counterbalanced by corresponding fearful advances in the other direction. New facilities for gaining wealth and for self-enjoyment ever stimulate not only the better, but also the worse propensities of our nature. Knowledge is power for evil, as well as for good. The leading race of men may do something towards the civilizing and teaching of the inferior races: but it generally has been found in history to have done more towards demoralizing and exterminating them. Its evil habits are greedily adopted, and carried on without limit or shame: its excesses become inveterate and suicidal; and its very diseases assume a more virulent and deadly type. And if it be answered, that though such may be the influence of a highly advanced civilization over one less advanced, yet in itself a leading race of men possesses power of continual advance in good,—the rejoinder in this may, I believe, be furnished by the history of such races as have from time to time taken the lead in the world. For has it not been found that, though for a time they have seemed the sources of blessing to our species, yet when tried by the only sure test, the test of time, they have themselves degenerated, and their place has been taken by others? If an example in our time were wanted, we could not point to one more remarkable than that which we are now witnessing on the other side of the Atlantic with regard to our own, the vaunted Anglo-Saxon race. What can be more signal than its present degradation, as we see it shewn in a return to all the unreasoning ferocity of the savage tribes, in the use of names and profession of motives sacred to the Christian and the man of peace, in justification of deeds their very opposites—in total disregard of truth public and private? Truly the lesson is there being taught us, if ever it was taught, that it is not by the influence of mere race that evil is kept in check among men: it is not because the blood of some races is better and purer than that of others, that more good has been predominant in one place and at one time, than elsewhere and at another time.

Nay, let us look back over what we have just been saying, and, if I am not mistaken, quite a different thought rises in our minds. With the height of civilization and of knowledge, as we have seen, evil tendencies are also developed to their height, and the dangers to social and moral well-being become greater. The better man becomes, the worse he becomes. And this is no paradox. The more light is shed abroad, the worse becomes the sin of those who prefer darkness to that increased light. The more men's hearts are penetrated and softened by good, from wheresoever arising, the more utterly lost to right feeling and humane affection must be that influence which would supersede that softening by a new and more impenetrable hardening.

And as connected with this thought, it is instructive to observe the precise way in which, though the good and the evil thus run on, so to speak, together, the whole result is for good and not for evil. The precise way, I say; for it is commonly not as we might expect, but far otherwise. The particular good which was in conflict with the evil is commonly overborne and destroyed by it. When, in a nation, good and evil influences are at issue with one another, the ordinary course is that the mischief prevails, and national ruin ensues. It has been so with all the great nations of antiquity; even with the specially favoured people of Israel. But the thing to be remarked is this: that when the good has been borne down and the evil has prevailed, then there arises to mankind out of the result a new and unlooked for good, far greater than that which has been lost. Through various great revolutions and catastrophes, all of them instances of the prevalence and victory of evil over good, our race has been brought forward, in a way which no human skill could have devised, from good to good. To call this accident, would be merely to confess ourselves unable to render a reason for it: would be simply to refuse to allow the same inference in this case which we should be compelled to allow in any similar one. And that inference, which the progress of our argument is now ripe for stating, is, and must surely be, this: that watching over the destinies of man, unseen by us, working in ways mysterious to us, checking and tempering the evil tendencies of men, and bringing good out of them, is a superior and all-wise Being, who is an enemy to evil and a friend to good.

This is the very least, surely, that any fair and reasonable mind can gather from the phenomena which we have been considering. And it is something, that this has been ever the general feeling of mankind; of the savage as well as the civilized, of the ignorant as well as the learned. All have concurred in feeling at the bottom of their hearts, that the influence which guides the helm of this world's affairs is not man himself, is not blind accident, but is a Power above man, and exercised continually over and in spite of man, with a wisdom and goodness which man cannot penetrate nor foresee. This I say is something. Compared with what we believe and know, it may be no very great thing: still it is enough to make the unbeliever and sceptic distrust his own view, when he finds all mankind against him.

But let us advance further. This Great Being who does good and loves the good, and whose face is against them that do evil,—do we know any more about Him, or is His existence and working only the inference of thinking minds from what they observe around them? Because, if so, it would seem after all, as if man himself were the cause of God doing any positive conscious good to the mind of man. If God is altogether dependent for recognition among men on man's finding Him out for himself, and if He has never personally interfered in the manifestation of Himself, it leaves us, though not exactly where we were, yet hardly, for any worthy purpose, at all advanced. Our next question then is, Has this Great Being, who thus mysteriously rules the destinies of man for good, ever manifested Himself to man? Has He ever deigned to look forth from the darkness which enwraps His counsels? Obviously this is a question which must be answered with extreme caution. Men are timid—are superstitious. They may mistake the workings of nature for His personal presence, or the ravings of madness for His prophetic voice, or the gathered wisdom of the shrewd or the aged among themselves for revelations from Him. We must look well to this, and must make our answer safe from being misled by these mistakes of men. Our answer then must be this, situated as we are, and believing what we do :—It is our belief, that this Being who rules over us for our good, and hates and averts our evil, has manifested Himself to us: has interfered personally in the affairs of the world, and uttered His voice to us. And this our belief rests not on any such insecure foundations as those just now disclaimed—not on mistakes which may have been made by the timid and superstitious, but on the fact and character of a permanent record being in existence of God's manifestation of Himself to men, which to our minds carries evidence of truth with it; and when looked at in itself, and compared with facts around us, proves to us that He has so manifested Himself.

But it may be said, though the Bible may not be the product of timidity or of mere superstition, how do we know that it has not been imposed upon us by designing persons, who have made God speak that which they would have Him say? Or again, how do we know that we have not in it merely the old stories and legends of a particular nation, gathered together by some wise and able hand, and imposed on the world as being what we suppose it to be? The great and final answer to all such questions must be found in that which I just now mentioned, the comparison of the Bible with facts around us. If, on doing this, it appear that it is totally unlike any other book on earth, and most of all unlike any books which have either set up for divine, or have recorded the primitive legends of the nations: if it appear that it is the only book in the world which tells us what the world is, and why it is, then it is at least matter for our serious consideration, whether it may not be that which it professes to be, a voice from One who is above the world, and guides the world. If, again, it be found that it is the only book in the world whose depths it is impossible to exhaust: that whereas every saying of human wisdom has an end and a circumference, may be seen through and surpassed, but the simplest saying of this book is inexhaustible by man, and enters on ground higher than he can attain unto, it may be worth our while to ask whether this be not evidence, that a wiser mind than any among the sons of men was at work in the writers of the Bible. Again,—and this is immediately to our present subject,—if we find, on examining this book, that He who professes to speak in it agrees in character with this same mighty, and good, and wise Being, who brings His good out of man's evil, it certainly would look to reasonable men as if the two, the Author of the Bible and the Ruler and Guide of mankind for good, were one and the same. But yet again: if we find that this is the only book in the world which speaks direct to the conscience and spirit of man: that all good, and all good men, have ever been found among those who value and believe in this book; and that when a man begins to doubt respecting it, when he surrenders his faith in it, when he allows human guidance to supersede it, from that time his moral being is affected for the worse,—we may well conclude that the book belongs to, and comes from, Him who is on the side of all good against all evil; in other words, that it is bound up with God, and God's rule among men, and the revelation of God's character to men.

To carry this argument no further, as not being our main one at present, God does in this book, which we have all reason to believe is His manifestation of Himself to us men, plainly declare the truth which we have been gathering from the aspect of the moral world around us—that He is the upholder of the good man against the evil man. "The eyes of the Lord are over the righteous, and His ears are open to his prayers: but the face of the Lord is against them that do evil." In all earthly matters we may take this for granted, that good is stronger than evil, and in the end shall prevail, because it has God on its side. Things shall not become worse and worse in the world taken as a whole; but even the apparent prevalence of evil in some portions, due to man's own depravity, shall be overruled by God for ultimate good. This is an immense comfort to every one who will look on it aright. It inspires courage in our efforts for good: it shews us that the issue is not always as we suppose it to be, but that very often there is good doing where we least know and suspect it.

And here again, passing from the mere general consideration of a belief in an overruling God to our belief in the God and Father of our Lord Jesus Christ, we shall find our grounds of comfort immensely strengthened, and our vision exceedingly cleared. During this present time, our ascended and glorified Saviour is waiting till all things are put under His feet. The whole moral world is by degrees being subdued to Him. By various dispensations of God's Providence, the good is prevailing, the evil is being defeated and put out. Now, if ever, is it true, that the good man is God's especial care, and that all scope is given for all the best and highest graces of humanity to expand and flourish. The perfect pattern of the Redeemer is before us; the witnessing Spirit is within us; the many mansions are being prepared for us, by Him who will return to take us thither. He that will love life and see good days, is not dependent on promises of earthly prosperity. His life is hid with Christ in God: his good days are to come in that place whither his Saviour Christ has gone before.

What a comfort it is for us to feel, in the midst of dark and perplexing circumstances, that the mighty and all-wise Being who is overruling all things for His glory, and bringing good out of man's evil, is our own God; that His covenanted mercies are ours; that in Christ Jesus all His promises are for ever ratified to each one, even the least and most helpless among us. What a powerful motive does it furnish to all good, what a discouragement from all evil, to remember that we have now no mere general assurance that God is on the side of good, but a positive promise, that all power in heaven and earth is given to Him, who laid down His life for the truth: and that one day, all who have followed Him in the paths of truth and holiness shall be like Him—partakers of His victory—changed into His spotless purity—inheritors of the new heaven and earth, wherein dwelleth righteousness; which He hath purchased for them, and wherein they shall reign with Him, when truth shall finally have been established, and all evil shall for ever have been put down.

IV.

DIVINE AND HUMAN AGENCY.

WHEN King David, after his sin in numbering the people, was offered his choice among three different modes of punishment, he replied (2 Sam. xxiv. 14), "Let us fall now into the hand of the Lord, for His mercies are great; and let me not fall into the hand of man." These words point to a tendency in the human mind, with reference to our belief in God's Providence, which it may be instructive to discuss and illustrate. I believe that some of our former meditations will throw light on it: and it in turn may perhaps make them better understood.

The habit is, that of less regarding God as acting on us and around us, when human agency is also employed, than when it is absent. We are apt, it is true, to be somewhat inconsistent here, as in other portions of our recognition of Providence; but here perhaps, as we before said in those cases, the inconsistency may be unavoidable, and may indeed be the only right path to pursue. A man comes to his death by the culpable negligence or want of foresight of a fellow-man. We regard that negligence or want of foresight as the assignable cause of his death. We say, if that matter had been better cared for,—if that dangerous path had been fenced, or that rail better laid, or that violent disease taken in time,—the man might have been alive now. Yet in the very next breath we say, that it pleased God to take him to Himself: and we deal with the fact of his death in terms which imply that no human power could have saved him. This double way of speaking remarkably illustrates the manner in which we find ourselves compelled to hold and proclaim both truths,—man's freedom of action and God's sovereign power of disposal. That the two here, as everywhere, seem inconsistent when brought into contact, is not a fault that we can help and correct, but a necessary consequence of the infirmity of our nature, and the narrowness of our comprehension. In reality, God just as much acts where men are concerned in bringing about the result; and men have just as much freedom of action where God overrules the result; but we cannot put the two together; we can only apprehend these truths separately. And separated, we do apprehend them; we speak of the event on one side as if man caused it, and on the other as if God pre-ordained it.

Now something of this unavoidable inconsistency is to be observed in the saying of David which I quoted, and perhaps a little more. Three things were offered to him, for his choice of one. "Shall seven years of famine come unto thee in thy land? or wilt thou flee three months before thine enemies while they pursue thee? or that there be three days' pestilence in thy land?"

First of all, the choice was given him by God Himself, in whose power it plainly lay to bring about any one of the three. The dearth, from which was to arise the famine: the war, which was to bring in the enemies: the seeds and access of the pestilence; all these were, by the very terms of the offer, to be of God's ordaining and bringing about. The hostile forces which were to pursue would be as much under His control as the disease, or the sun and the clouds. Whichsoever of the three befell the penitent king, he would still fall into the hands of God, and not of man. What then, in his estimation, made the difference? I may say, what would make it in our own? for I doubt not that we all feel the same as he did. Is it not this—that in the one case man *appears* as the agent, whereas in the two others he does not appear, but God only? We may say that the answer, though a beautiful one, is one indicative of weak faith; that if the king had been strong in faith, he would equally have seen himself safe in the great mercies of God, whether man intervened between God and himself or not. And doubtless this is so; but even though the faith may be weak, it is, I believe, not only one which we are obliged to be contented with, but of that sort which God means us to have. All that happens to us is naturally and necessarily divided off by us into these two classes of events: those which are man's doing, and those which are God's doing. The merchant insures his ship, or undertakes safely to convey the merchandise entrusted to him: and in so doing, he speaks of "the act of God;" meaning, the storm which may imperil, or the calm which may detain his vessel. Inquiry is made into the cause of a death, and if it has been sudden, or unassignable, it is said to have taken place "by the visitation of God."

Let us follow out our habits of this kind a little further. It appears also, that in great and solemn matters we are more ready to acknowledge the interposition of God, than in ordinary and less significant ones; even where the difference of the presence or absence of human agency does not occur. We do not scruple to say in any society, that escape from accident, or recovery from grievous sickness, has been providential. All acquiesce in one sentiment, and even the scorner's brow is for once relaxed into approval. But if the same merciful preservation has extended to the prevention of accident altogether, or to the long maintenance of health uninterrupted, we do not equally characterize these as the act of God, but almost take them as matters of course; and we should pass with the world for enthusiasts or weak-minded persons, if we spoke otherwise about them. This practice, though seemingly different from that other, is in reality the same. As long as the world goes on without any interruption to its ordinary course, we seem to have no reason to attribute that course to anything beyond ordinary agencies, which appear to us as if they always had been, and always would continue to be; but when there comes an interruption in the slightest degree unlooked for, then we begin to speak of Divine Providence, and to see God interfering. This last fact is remarkably illustrated by remembering that sometimes our recognition or non-recognition of God's Hand takes place without any reference to the relative importance of events, but entirely with reference to their usual or unusual character. The rising of the sun each morning by the revolution of the earth on her axis,—the bringing in of summer and winter by the inclination of that axis,—the drawing over us of the cloud from which descends the fertilizing shower,—these are in reality immeasurably greater events, and more eloquent of divine power, than many things in which we all see and acknowledge the present hand of God. Yet in these we never see it, or even speak of it. Sometimes, indeed, when Nature's operations assume a startling or terrifying character, we seem compelled to see God acting in them. The thunderings and lightnings of the overcharged air, the storm by which the balance of the atmosphere is restored, these seem to us evident proofs of God's interference: whereas that interference is in reality as much proved by the opening of the bud, or by the withering of the herbage after continued drought. We cannot see this matter as it really is, but only as it is relatively to ourselves. For every event our minds strive to supply some agent: if we see man, if we see the ordinary laws of nature at work by our side, we are apt to look no further, and to seek for no higher cause: but if all is blank, and the result only is seen, then we seem to rise upward in thought through the empty heavens, till we come to the Throne and Him that sitteth thereon. This is one form of the feeling induced by our infirmity. And another is, as we have partly seen, that as long as all is quiet, and our minds are not unusually excited, we are content to look no further than natural causes; but the moment our fears are aroused, the moment we are anyhow deeply stirred in spirit, we see and we acknowledge Him in whose hands are all our ways.

Let us go on to speak of the use, and of the abuse, of this practice. Doubtless it has its beneficent use, or God would not have so universally implanted it in our nature—in the best and godliest of men, as well as in those who regard Him not. And I think this use is not difficult to ascertain. "We walk by faith, not by sight." But it is plain that while this is true, it can be true only of the main turnings of our course, not of every step at every time. The evidence of our senses must be our guide in a world which is apprehended by our senses, and faith in things unseen must come in where the world around us threatens to overbear our higher principles and instincts. If a man always, and day by day, guided every portion of his course by consciousness of the things unseen, and not according to the things seen, he would become a dreamer, and would be unfit to move and act in this working-day world. And just so in the case which we are considering. The constant thought and recognition of God is good, is necessary for us all, who would live for any worthy purpose.

> "Happy the man who sees a God employed
> In all the good and ill that chequers life."

But to refer every ordinary matter, every insignificant result, to Him as its immediate agent, would on the one hand bring in superstition and morbid fancy, and on the other would tend to diminish our reverence for God Himself. It would bring in superstition and morbid fancy: for it would lead us ever to be looking for the Almighty hand in those minute details of its working, which are concealed from us; and we should be attributing to God our own petty ways of acting, and our own insufficient and unworthy motives. We should be ever regarding ourselves as His chiefly favoured ones, and the misfortunes of others as attributable to His vengeance for that in them which is faulty in our eyes. The last dread famine in Ireland was at one and the same time regarded by Protestants as a judgment on Popery, and by Romanists as a judgment on the land for the success of Protestant missions. Such a circumstance should teach us caution, and shew us that it is sometimes good to withhold our decision on the purposes and workings of God's Providence. It does not become soberminded Christians, who believe that He doeth all things well, to betake themselves to finding fault with His arrangements, if the showers fall more or less frequently than usual, or if a partial blighting of the fruits of the earth diminish the prosperity of one particular portion of our globe. The exceptional weather which spoils a harvest, may be His means of averting a pestilence; and the calamity which causes one branch of industry to stagnate, may be a call from Him to waken thenceforth better and higher energies of a people. We must not judge Him, but trust Him. His hand is too large for us to see all it does at once; its very opening to shed on us the blessings with which it is loaded may crush some frail image on which we think our well-being depends. Extreme sensitiveness to God's acts is not true resignation to His will.

Again, I said, that such minute apportionment of all things to His immediate agency tends to diminish reverence for Him. This indeed would follow from its producing superstition; for where there is superstition, there cannot be reverence. But it is also very plain on other grounds. "God is in heaven, and thou on earth," says the Holy Spirit in Scripture: "therefore let thy words be few." That is, not only let thy prayer be short, and sober, and reverent,—avoiding the familiarity induced by many words,—but the meaning doubtless extends further, to this,—let thy surmises and sayings about God and His acts be few, and certain, and reverent also. It has not pleased Him to move visibly among us, nor to hold converse with us face to face. We look before us, and He is not there; and behind us, but we cannot perceive His presence. He withholds Himself from us, that we may adore Him, and magnify Him in our thoughts. When it became necessary, in His great purposes, that He should be seen by man on earth, men did not reverence Him, but they despised Him, and cruelly entreated Him. His ways are not our ways: when we make them our ways, we so far degrade Him. The poor Papist, who has a saint for every turn in life, falls to cursing his saints, when those turns are not to his advantage. He who is not content without seeing God everywhere, would, from the very infirmity of our constitution, reverence Him nowhere. So that it is a good and wise provision of Him who made us, that men in general are not given to morbid and minute tracing of His working in ordinary life. Their thoughts about Him are thus kept within the bounds of sobriety and due reverence, and are attuned to the feelings towards Him which He would have us entertain; so that when we are brought face to face with Him, we meet Him with becoming awe, and abase ourselves in dust and ashes.

But the tendency and the practice bring with them their abuse likewise. And that abuse consists in this, that we are too often given to forget God altogether, where man is concerned. It is not easy to acquit David himself of something like this fault. If enemies were to pursue him while he fled before them, it seemed to him as if he would be exposed to all the fury and all the caprice of man's vindictive agency. And so it is very often with us. We look too much to man, we put too much confidence in human agents. We hope for prosperity, or we fear thwarting, and the access of adversity, simply and entirely from man, forgetting that to every man on earth God says, "Hitherto shalt thou go, but no further." And this evil habit of forgetting God extends far wider than the mere looking to man for good or evil

Thousands among ourselves, not unbelievers by profession, pass through the realities of life without a thought of God and His sovereign disposal of them. Their course day by day, and year by year, is led without any consciousness that they are in his Almighty hand. I don't mean that they never pray, or never go to church; but that in the inner chamber of their hearts, where plans are made, and where joys and sorrows have their source, God is not present; their springs of life are godless, and they have lost all that can make life worth living.

Another abuse of the habit of which I am treating is, a bold and presumptuous spirit, which not only leaves out God, but openly despises Him, as taking no part in human affairs. This may not seem to be common; but it is in fact far more common than we suppose. Legendary history is full of stories illustrating the punishment of such presumption. We will take but one, and that for the sake of putting clearly before us the spirit which I mean. It is that, repeated in various forms at different places on our island coast, of the merchant adventurer now in sight of land after a prosperous voyage, and reminded that he owes thanks to God for his safety, and that of his charge. "Nay," he replies, "thank the good ship and the fair wind." And then in the story, the bank of clouds gathers in the West, and the vengeance of Him who was neglected descends on the ship and her captain, and the pious adviser alone escapes to tell the tale. These stories may or may not be themselves matters of fact: but they point to a great fact in the habits of ordinary men: a confidence in self and in human skill, and a casting off of God as the disposer of the issues of our actions. It is not that we can afford to dispense with any human effort of diligence or skill; these are God's appointed means of working among us and by us; but it is, that as He is pleased not to work without these, so these must not be calculated on without taking into account His works, apart from which they are of no avail. The advice of the old Puritan general to his soldiers, to trust in God and keep their powder dry, was, homely as it may seem, sound and good. He would be equally wrong who, professing to trust in God, let his powder get wet, with him who took the proper precaution, but left God out of his calculation. Among men of the world, among those engaged in business and working for this world's wealth, the latter fault is much the more common of the two. We do not remember God as we ought. Things here stand in His place, and veil Him from our sight. We take into account everything else first, and Him last: or far too often, Him not at all.

But let us recur, in drawing our meditation to a close, to the real comfort to be derived from the habit which we have been considering, in cases where nothing stands between us and the Almighty hand. It may be a weakness to recognise God more in these than in others; but it is a weakness wherein is strength and consolation. When the frame gives way under sickness, and the foundations of life are sapped; when calamity over which we have no control desecrates our homes and hearts; when our flesh and heart fail, not because of man, but because of One greater than man, who is pleading with us face to face; is it not mercifully ordained, that in all such cases the universal tendency is to see God working, to acknowledge ourselves to be in His hand, to feel that His mercies are over all, and are great?

And is it not also a mercy, that we all feel what David did, that it is God, and not man, whom we wish to have for the disposer of our fate? that from the infirmity and caprice of our fellow-creatures we are ever glad to take refuge with Him whose mercies are great, and who we know doeth all things well?

We feel, that man may mistake us, man may deal unjustly and unkindly with us, man may serve his own purposes at our expense, man may be wanting in sympathy, in equity, in lenity: but none of these can be with Him whose tender mercies are over all His works: the Judge of all the earth must be just: the Saviour of mankind must care for those whom He bought with His blood: the blessed Spirit of God will not easily forsake nor reprobate those with whom it is His sacred office to dwell and to plead continually.

"Let us fall into the hand of the Lord, for His mercies are great: and let us not fall into the hand of man."

V.

EFFECT ON MEN OF GOD'S ORDINARY AND EXTRAORDINARY DEALINGS.

OUR Lord, in the remarkable parable of the rich man and Lazarus, puts into the mouth of Abraham, the Father of the faithful, this saying: that if the rich man's brethren believed not Moses and the Prophets, neither would they be persuaded though one were to rise from the dead: in other words, that if the ordinary means of grace are powerless upon a man's heart and life, the extraordinary judgments of God will be powerless also.

Let us, in this meditation, apply this declaration of our Lord (for it is manifestly delivered under His sanction, and for us) to ourselves. Let us do so in the manner in which we have been, in our other meditations, attempting to deal with sacred truths and their application: by a matter of fact examination into the things which actually happen in our own hearts and lives. Let us in this manner try to make the truth of our Lord's saying apparent, and to force it in upon our thoughts as a reality. The form which our inquiry will take is this: What is the effect on men's minds of the ordinary means of grace and course of God's providence? What again is the effect on men's minds of God's exceptional and extraordinary judgments? And then combining the two together, we shall try to show that if the former effect do not succeed in changing the life, it is not likely that the latter will do so.

First then, what is the effect on men's minds of the ordinary means of grace and course of God's providence? What might we expect it to be, from the very nature of those things and of the minds of men? Let us look at any human character: our own individual character, for instance. What have been the greatest and most lasting effects ever produced on it? How is it, in other words, that we come to be what we now find ourselves? Let us examine, in any case, into some habit which has grown up in us, so that it is a part of our very self. How came it about? We can trace it to constant insensible influence of some kind, and mostly to influence exerted in early life. And when we come to add together a multitude of these influences exerted on us from without and from within, and take into account circumstances which have lain all round us throughout life, we arrive at something like a reason for the greater part of the habits, and likings, and dislikes, and desires, and tendencies of our individual character. These grew up by degrees; we could not trace their growth day by day—hardly year by year: but when we look at the scenes amidst which we lived, and the persons with whom our lot was cast, and, to use a Scripture expression, the times that went over us, we see, taking a large and general view, how each of these habits and propensities must have grown up, even though we could not trace it. Now just such, I believe, is the usual effect of the ordinary means of grace and calls of God's providence, where they affect men at all. The case where they do not is not at present under consideration, but will be by-and-by. Where a man is affected by them, their working is of this gentle, gradual, deep kind. His life becomes cast into their mould: his daily thoughts run in the channels of their great onward flows and tendencies; his actions take colour from this cast and complexion of his thoughts. It is here as it is with all matters of habit. The man whose days have been spent in the plains cannot be inured to mountain climbing, nor are the forms and phenomena of mountain scenery familiar to his thoughts and imaginations: take him to the hill country, and all would be strange to him. But to the child of the mountains all these things are matter of course, however wonderful they may be in themselves. The masses of vast and shadowy rock, the clouds resting halfway down the mountain side, the torrent ever sounding in its impetuous strength, the cataract with its rainbow,—these, which are wonders to others, are the very materials of daily life to him. The plainsman wearies, and calls for rest, with a few hours' breasting of the hill track, up which his daily work has carried the mountaineer, till his very frame has knit into aptitude for the task. And not otherwise is it with the effect on men's minds of the ordinary means of grace and course of God's providence. Those miracles of Divine goodness, which make up the history of redemption, become a portion of the very life itself. Difficulties which surpass human comprehension, constitute the daily path and walk of faith and holy practice. Where the unaccustomed step would falter, and the muscles would immediately weary, the habituated believer goes on his way fearless and contented. The thews and sinews of his mind, so to speak, have gathered the requisite strength,—and he can climb the crag without murmuring and without weariness: his eye has been long used to the abyss underlying his vision, and he can gaze down from the cliff-path without giddiness. Effects of this kind are not half enough taken into account among us. They are, for us who have grown up from childhood in the faith, our greatest mercies, and our most precious possessions. Take any of the great doctrines on which the life of the Church is built: the Incarnation, the Atonement, the indwelling of the Spirit, or any other; present such a doctrine to the unaccustomed mind, and what is the effect? Look up at yonder mountain side. Do you see that track zigzagging along the face, as it appears, of the perpendicular rock? It glitters, as you look, in the sun, moist and slippery with the never-failing mists. What human foot could venture thither in safety? Yet day by day along that path passes the woodman, singing as he goes to his work; yet day by day along that dizzy track gaily pass his little children with their father's mid-day meal, sportively plucking the bright blossoms that peep from under the patches of snow. Even so is it with the blessed doctrines on which the soul lives and works in God's Church. To the unbeliever they are full of difficulties—they seem impossible: he gazes on them, and wonders that any can receive them and work in their strength: but to him who has grown in their presence and been accustomed to their power, they are things familiar, and their difficulties do not present themselves: their majesty has passed into his spirit, and their living efficiency has long wrought within him. And we may well believe that it is for this reason, among others, that it has pleased the Lord that reception into His Church by Holy Baptism should not wait for the mature understanding, but should be the very first thing in life: in order that the blessed effects of His mighty Love for us should be produced at the greatest possible advantage: in order that "Heaven" may "lie about us in our infancy," and holy and saving truth may be carried into our young minds long before we are aware of its presence. To the Christian child, no playfellow of earliest years is closer to memory and affection, than the Child of Bethlehem: no tales of wonder more familiar, than the miracles of the Saviour's mercy: to him, the Cross, and the Tomb, and the Resurrection morning, and the ascending up into heaven, and the sitting at the right hand of God, are no strange things, to be questioned by the doubting reason, and mastered by the understanding: but have formed, from his earliest recollection, the very clothing and inhabitation of his thoughts.

One word, before we pass to our next point, on the outward effect produced now, and continually, on us who believe, by the ordinary means of grace and course of Providence. And here, it may be conceived, the result of inquiry will be almost insensible. Between two men, both brought up as Christians, both holding the faith, both living correct and blameless lives, but one a regular attendant at public worship, a constant reader of his Bible, and the other a neglecter of both, what difference can we perceive? The question, it seems to me, is just as if it were asked respecting two buildings, both outwardly complete, in one of which the work of fitting and adorning was diligently carried on, while in the other it was utterly neglected. In outward appearance, both are the same. The mere passer-by knows no difference between the two. But enter within: see the two houses as any one sees them who knows their inmost recesses, and how vast is the real difference! The one is gradually preparing for the master's use; the other is a mere shell, worthless for human habitation. Or let us take the same truth in the very illustration given by our Lord Himself. Ten virgins went out to meet the bridegroom. Five had provided for delay, and had taken care to be ready whenever He should come: five had made no provision. Here we have before us just the difference in question. All these are Christian souls, come out from the world into the waiting Church of Christ: and our Lord in the parable sets before us the difference between those who by the use of the means of grace make continual preparation for His coming, and those who make no such preparation. The effect of these ordinary means of grace is, to fit and adorn the soul for God's work, and for God's summons to Himself;

to supply the waste and wear of daily contact with the world, that there may be oil in the vessel, when the cry is made, that the Bridegroom cometh. He who pays regard to God's ordinances, will find the blessing when he needs it most; he who neglects them, will find himself, at that hour, all unprepared. And it will be well if he be not shut out, in the day when the Lord gathers His people.

Such then seems to be the effect on men of the ordinary means of grace and the calls and advices of God's providence, when they are listened to and received into the heart.

And now let us ask ourselves, what is the effect on men's minds of God's exceptional and extraordinary judgments? Let us see what we mean by these terms. The parable to which we referred in the beginning gives us a notable example: the rising of one from the dead. But though this exactly suited the case in the parable, it will not suit ours, because we do not now see around us such

ON PROVIDENCE. 215

exercise of divine power as the raising of the dead. And manifestly it will not do to say, that there are as great miracles going on around us, if men would consider and perceive them: for by the very nature of the case we want for our present purpose something which men *cannot help* perceiving, and being affected by. Still, the instance in the parable will guide us to the *kind* of incident of which we are in search. Anything which is unusual, and breaks in on the ordinary daily course of events assumed as likely to happen, is of the kind which we seek: especially if it bear a character of solemnity, and carry a serious thought down into a man whether he will or no. Of such a kind, for example, is the occurrence of a death in the midst of us; a sudden interposition of One who is able to make things about us to be as He wills, and not as we will. And this is perhaps the commonest instance of God's extraordinary judgments, happening as it does every day somewhere, and many times in the experience of us all among our own kinsfolk and acquaintance. Now what is the usual effect of such an event on men's minds? We may give two answers to the question: first as regards those who are affected by the ordinary means of grace, and course of God's providence,—and then as regards those who are not affected by them. What is the effect on us who believe, of such an event as that which we have mentioned? I mean, the effect on our religious lives and on our own characters? Of course there are various degrees of sorrow and regret, as we approached nearer in intimacy or friendship to any one who is taken from us: and these must not be altogether left out; for all sorrow is a power over the soul, and brings a lull within, during which the voice of God may be heard. But I mean principally, what is the abiding effect on our religious lives, on our watchfulness for a like summons in our own case, on our estimate of this world and of eternity, on our thoughts of other men and of ourselves? Doubtless, if we be men really in earnest, there is an effect: and O thank God for it. But of what kind? If I mistake not, in our case, just of the same kind, allowing for necessary differences, as that of the ordinary means of grace and occurrences of life. As with them it would be impossible to say what part each service, each Holy Communion, each day's more experience of God's works and ways, bore in the building up and fitting the Christian character,—and yet we know that each did bear some part: so is it ever likewise with these extraordinary judgments of God. They pass over us; for a short time thought is solemnized, and exuberant spirits are checked, and we feel this life less secure, and another life more real and nearer to us: and then time goes by, and the past event, like all past events, comparatively loses its power: present and ordinary things flow in, and resume their influences over us; and, to outward seeming, all is again as if the judgment had not been. There is, nevertheless, as I said, a certain abiding effect: but like that other, it is gradual, and insensible, and accumulative; by the recurrence of these warnings we become manifestly and insensibly more prepared against our own time: by the recurrence of sorrow the heart is softened: by the recurrence of kindly and sympathising feelings we have gentler thoughts of others, and less selfish ones about our own likings and interests. But all this result is produced, let it be remembered, on hearts already believing, already predisposed by habit to be turned in the direction of God's preventing and warning grace: and again, all this is produced, not by the sudden and overwhelming force of the event itself, but in spite of that force being notoriously evanescent, and having seemingly been exerted in vain.

And if we now pass on to the matter most

directly at issue, and ask, what effect will God's exceptional and extraordinary judgments produce, on one who neglects or refuses to hear the ordinary means of grace and calls of Providence? our answer will surely not be doubtful nor difficult. On the occurrence of one of those judgments, his thoughts, like those of the other, will be solemnized for a time. There is not a heart so light, or a life so worldly, but the sound of the death-bell carries on it some grave reminding, however unwelcome, and however dissimulated. But what is the effect in after time? For good, absolutely nothing. The gentle gradual influence, which in the other case remained after the first shock had passed away, does not in this case exist at all: the man is unaccustomed to the daily warnings and remindings of grace and instruction: his heart is essentially hard, and the repeated and undecided shocks of judgments of this kind only harden it still more. No sinner is so hardened, as one who lives in the midst of warnings and terror. Incredible as it may seem, we read that no robbers are so brutal, no murderers so pitiless, as those who wander among the wounded after a battle, where every scene of suffering, one would think, would be enough to melt the stoutest heart. Again, it is well known that the habitual sight of anguish and pain is apt, in ordinary persons, to steel the heart against sympathy with both. And if such be the outward effect, so transitory, so powerless for good, so likely to produce even permanent mischief by repetition, shall we find any inward influence exerted on the heart of the careless and impenitent by these exceptional interferences of God's hand? Even in our own time, even with our Lord's warning words before us, we often hear these events spoken of as if they had power to convert the sinner. It would be presumption to say, that God may not make use of any means for this purpose: but it would, on the other side, be idle to shut our eyes to the plain facts of His dealings with men: and one of those plain facts is, that He does not ordinarily make use of events of this kind for that purpose. They who do not listen to the ordinary means of grace, do not, as a matter of fact, listen to these. The sinner who turns a deaf ear to the church-bell, turns a deaf ear to the death-bell also, as far as any permanent good is concerned. Let us strengthen the inference by an example; by *the great* example from history. The Jews heard not Moses and the Prophets. The law spoke of justice, mercy, and the love of God: they were unjust, and unmerciful, and ungodly, rejecting Him whom God had sent, and refusing to see the testimony of His blameless life and holy words. He raised up one from the dead, in the presence of many of their chief men. And what do we read of the effect on them? "The Pharisees consulted that they might put Lazarus also to death; that because of him many went away and believed in Jesus." And afterwards the Son of God

Himself went unto them from the dead, His resurrection being assured to them by the testimony of those who had seen and heard and handled Him, after He was risen. But in all this, they did not believe: they refused the evidence, they persecuted the followers of Jesus, their city and temple miserably perished, and they are scattered over the earth unto this day.

Such was the fulfilment of our Lord's saying in them to whom it was spoken: and of that same kind will it ever be in all men under similar circumstances. If we will not listen to the ordinary means of grace; if the course of God's warning and loving Providence have no teaching for us;—then not unusual judgments, not the occurrence of death among us, no, nor of sickness and the approach of death to ourselves, will produce the effect which the others could not. These solemn judgments, these startling calls, are full of instruction: but it is to those who are under God's teaching, not to those who refuse it, and put it behind them. Conversion and sanctification, life and growth in grace, are to be found in the ordinary services of the Church, and reading of God's word, and seeking to Him day by day; where these are not, none of God's extraordinary calls will waken the sleeping soul.

VI.

GOD'S ESTIMATE OF HIS OWN WORKS.

In resuming our meditations on the Providence of God, one very interesting inquiry presents itself to us. How does the Creator and Redeemer of nature look upon His own creation? What relative value in His eyes have the various ranks and orders of His creatures? Is it possible, that we men may be wrong in believing ourselves to be the flower and crown of His works on earth? As we know that within the limits of our own race He esteems the lowly more than the proud, may it not be even so outside the limits of our own race,—that proud *man*, who ever puts himself foremost in creation, may after all be in the sight of God of less account than some tribe of God's creatures far beneath him in power and intelligence?

The answer to this question cannot be unimportant to us. If our own view of our place in creation be confirmed to us by our Lord's own words and arguments, the fact of that confirmation, and the manner in which He is pleased to make the announcement, and the lessons which He draws and which we may draw from it, must be alike edifying and profitable.

Our Lord devotes the second portion of His great Sermon on the Mount to the enforcing on us of a simple and undivided heart in matters pertaining to God. Following in that discourse the process of the Spirit's work on man as afterwards described by Himself, and first dealing with the convictions and measures of sin,—He next comes to His description of the righteousness of those who would be His disciples, and ends by giving them His rules for their judgment of men and things about them. It is in this middle portion, that the passage occurs which deals with the question before us. Having told us that our righteousness is not to be done before men to be seen of them, but is to be such as has real existence before our Father who seeth in secret, He then tells us that no man can serve two masters, God and this present world. The soul of man, whichever way drawn and tending, " moveth altogether, if it move at all." . The man who pretends divided service, who thinks that he can afford to have one eye towards God and the next life, and the other towards self and this life, will find in the end that he has been mistaken, that he has not been doing himself good by his attempt, which seemed so shrewd and worldly-wise, but evil: that he has been trying to live under impossible conditions, and the result has been the break up and ruin of his eternal prospects, in the demoralization of his conscience and his inner being.

All this is important to our present consideration, because our Lord passes to the portion in which our question is treated with a " Therefore I say unto you," implying that what follows is grounded on what went before. And so indeed it is. If the heart and the service of the life will not bear dividing, then the thoughts of the heart about a man's daily maintenance and welfare must not, while he professes to believe in and depend on God, be anxiously distracted, partly trusting Him and partly distrusting Him. "Therefore I say unto you, Take not anxious thought for your life, what you shall eat; nor for your raiment, what ye shall put on." I may remark, in passing, that the English reader is apt to be misled in this passage by the rendering of our version, "Take no thought," which does not represent what our Lord says, and would, as we now understand the words, be both impossible to carry out, and contradictory

ON PROVIDENCE. 227

to other express commands of Holy Scripture. The original word thus rendered signifies, taking anxious, distracted care. It is derived from a verb which means to divide into two or more parts: and is thus admirably suited to describe the sort of care which will not suit him whose heart is to be single and undivided in the service of his Father in heaven. This division of heart, this distracted and distrustful care, we Christians are not to allow in ourselves with regard to our subsistence, or to our necessary shelter and due adornment of the body. And why? for here comes in the treatment of the question which we proposed to ourselves in the outset. And let me remark, that there is a peculiar and delightful interest about this part of our Lord's discourse. Wherever, in the high teaching of inspiration, Creation and Redemption are brought together, there is a charm in the words which goes to every heart, and impresses them on every mind. Who, for instance, does not feel this in that wonderful eighth chapter to the Romans, where the Apostle assures us, that all creation around is waiting and sighing for the glorious day when our bodies shall be clothed with immortality? And if so, assuredly here also will this be the case, where the Son of God, the Lord of Creation, is pleased to afford us a glimpse of His own estimate of portions of His works which we see about us, and to describe to us those beauties and adornments of His inferior creatures of which He alone knows the secret and the value. "Behold," He says, "the birds of the air; they sow not, neither do they reap, nor gather into barns; yet your heavenly Father feedeth them." The first argument here is of an absolute kind: the second of a relative kind. First, our Lord says, Observe, how large a portion of Creation is absolutely dependent on the unsolicited and spontaneous goodness of your heavenly Father. These creatures live in wild liberty, giving no care to provide stores for distant time: they are provisionless and defenceless: but He whom you serve, and whose children you are, provides for them. He has endowed them with instinct, guided by which they go in search of their daily food: and year by year and day by day His bounty provides that that food shall lie scattered where they may find it. Will One so careful, and so bountiful, suffer *any* portion of His creatures to go neglected by Him? Cannot you trust the bountiful and loving Father who feeds the birds of the air? So far for the direct and absolute argument: to which it might perhaps have been answered by one willing to argue for argument's sake, that we are not so sure that we are equally with them the objects of our heavenly Father's care. But our Lord precludes all such distrustful escapes from His inference, by appealing at once to our sense of our place in creation as compared with theirs, and He adds, "*Are ye not much better than they?*" Our superiority to them is not a matter requiring proof, but a conviction at once to be assumed and appealed to. Now, as I said in the beginning, the fact of our Lord's thus confirming our view of our place in creation is something. Let our persuasion of an obvious truth be ever so strong, we cannot but feel that our hold on it is firmer, when we hear it asserted by the God of truth.

We are better than they. Now, as far as our outward sight goes, we and they perish by a common fate. Their bodies and ours moulder together in the dust of the earth. But we are better than they. Better, not as regards what we see, this common fate, this common decay. No: if that only be considered, we are much worse than they. We have thoughts and hopes reaching forward into immortality: they have none. If we are to perish with them, bitter is our lot: sad indeed the cutting off of high aspirations, and bright hopes and eager yearnings. If in this life only we have hope in Christ, we are of all Creation the most miserable. How then are we so much better than they? How can we be so very sure that the great Father who neglects not them, will not forget nor neglect us? How, but by this—that we have a life which they have not; that the fate which overtakes us and them is common to us both, as far as the outward eye reaches, but that beyond, there is for us a life which is not for them: that the decay in which our bodies and theirs moulder together is not for us what it is for them: that our dust shall arise, while theirs shall remain? Here is our real superiority: here is the truth by which the Lord's argument is driven home to our convictions: the life to come; the life that now is, a preparation for the life to come. If God so takes care of these fleeting and ephemeral creatures, who endure but for an hour of the great day of the world, how much more will He take care of those whose life is not limited by the duration of the creation itself—who shall survive the wreck of matter and the crash of worlds!

But there is more yet behind. Mere immortality confers a superior rank over that which is mortal: still mere immortality may be a curse, and not a blessing. But you know, that that which it cost to make it a blessing, God Himself has paid for us. And in another part of the New Testament, we have this very fact used as an argument tending in the same direction as this which we are considering. "He who spared not His own Son, but delivered Him up for us all, shall He not, with Him, also freely give us all things?"

Such is the absolute, and such is the relative argument here used. God, who feedeth the birds of the air, will not neglect any portion of His creatures: God, who feedeth with tender care an inferior tribe of His creatures, will not neglect nor forget one far better than it. We may safely trust our daily sustenance and welfare in His hands, as long as we do not cast ourselves out of the course of His providential care by an indolent, or a proud, or a reckless repudiation of the work which He has given us to do. "Seek ye first the kingdom of God and

His righteousness :" be found, that is, in the place where He has put you, and fulfilling its duties as accountable to Him, and seeking to know Him and please Him, and all needful things shall be added to you.

But there is a second portion of our cares and anxieties, to which our Lord applies the same argument. Food is the first necessity of life; the second is clothing. And here enters an element which, not properly belonging to the actual supply of the want, has yet become mixed up with it, and has come to form a considerable part of our cares respecting it. Our clothing is not only for shelter and decorum, but it is also for adornment. A disposition to deck the person is natural to all mankind. And let it be noticed that our Lord, who knows what is in man, takes up and recognises this as a part in dealing with this portion of our wants. He does not repudiate it nor chide it down. Had He been here employed in giving us cautions as to its moderation and its excess, there can be no doubt that He would have said, even as His Apostle Peter has said, that it becomes not us to place our chief adornment in outward things applied to the body, but in the hidden man of the heart. There within, ought to be the purest tints, there the choicest jewels. But it is not His practice in His divine teaching, to look aside, or go out of the way, to inculcate caution. It is rather His habit, generously to recognise, and with sympathy to speak of, those tendencies which God has implanted in us for good, and thereby to teach us to look on them as good, and to keep them pure and good, and to use them for good. And such a use, there can be no doubt, we are able to make, and by far the greater part of us do make, of this universal tendency to personal adornment. Its excess is foolish and sinful: its moderate use is not only lawful but beneficial, inasmuch as it tends to carry out the designs of God's providence in the social state in which we live. Large classes of the teeming population of the civilized earth are dependent for their living on the demand for fabrics tending to minister to this propensity for adornment. We are not intended to thwart, but to fall in with, that arrangement. The line of duty in this matter is already marked for all who will be not unwise, but understanding what the will of the Lord is. The vain and frivolous on the one hand, the ill-balanced mind and morbid conscience on the other, will stray out of it; but for most of us there is little danger: public opinion, guided and corrected by Christian intelligence, prescribes the mean; and, generally speaking, it is observed.

So then our Lord takes for granted this our need and the further tendency which accompanies it, and He argues respecting both, much in the same way as before. He forbids us to entertain anxious or distracting thoughts on the question, wherewithal we are to be clothed. Doubtless, in the simple state of society found in that land, and at that time, this anxious care was more visible on the surface than it can be in our artificial condition. There, the mother of the household is described to us as spending her time at the distaff and the loom: and the choice of pattern and colour, the preparation of the material and the dye, and many other details which we in our homes are now spared, must have vastly enhanced the danger of making this question the cause of distracting and mischievous anxiety.

But here, as before, the Lord takes an example from creation around us. "Consider," He says, "the lilies of the field, how they grow: they toil not, neither do they spin: yet I say unto you that even Solomon in all his glory was not arrayed like one of these." Wonderful indeed is such a sentence from Him who created all things, and whose glory fills the Universe. Wonderful, to hear Him giving us His own estimate of the relative splendour of the richest adornment that man can devise, and the symmetry and colours of the wayside flower. And observe that this second argument, though in the main of the same kind as the former, yet differs somewhat from it in the manner of application. Then it was, if God feeds the inferior and less worthy tribe of His creatures, shall He not much more feed you who are so far better than they? The difference, on which that argument rested, was one between the two classes brought into comparison: that which God so freely and constantly ministers to the less important class, we may safely assume He will as freely and constantly furnish to ourselves. But here, the difference on which the argument rests is of another kind. It is not between the two classes treated of, the flowers and ourselves, —but between the degrees of perfection attained in the result sought for. In the other case, we had simply the fact of the feeding: here, we have the degree of adornment. God clothes the lilies, as never man in his pomp, as never woman in her beauty, was yet bedecked. One of these wayside flowers, if we could see all the secrets and all the blendings of its colours, if we could penetrate all the laws which regulate the symmetry and elegance of its form, if we could appreciate all the care bestowed by the Creator on the delicacy and complexion of its texture, would put all human adornment to shame. If we try one of these with the power of the microscope,—the more we magnify it, the more glories of form and colour, the more intricate symmetries of texture, astonish the dazzled eye: subject to the same test the most delicately-woven fabric of human skill, the most precise and uniform artificial application of colour, and as it expands before the scrutiny, it degenerates into a coarse and unseemly mass, daubed as if by an unskilful hand. He who has lavished all this exquisite skill on the rank growth of the field, which is flourishing to-day, and cut down and dried up and burnt to-morrow, shall He not much more clothe you, O ye of little faith? Will not He, in His good Providence, bring about for all of us who serve Him and seek to do His will, a sufficient and seemly supply of what is needful and what is becoming for the clothing of the body? We are to trust Him with the sustenance of our lives, we are to trust Him with sheltering and arraying us. We are better employed than that we ought to distract our thoughts day by day about these matters: we have no time to bestow on them as life's business: they must not eat out the spirit of a sound and earnest mind,—they must not unteach us self-denial, they must not be clamouring when we ought to be listening to the whisper of sympathy and God's spirit: they must not ever be rising as drifts of clouds, troubling the clear morning of the Christian's day, and blotting the Sun of Righteousness by whose light he walks and works.

This it is, and no impossible, no exaggerated casting away of earthly cares which the Lord requires of us. It is the knowing what we are, and who cares for us, and acting in that knowledge. It is told of the great Cæsar, that being at sea in a storm, and beholding the shipman unmanned with fear, he cried, "Fear not; thou hast Cæsar on board." This was perhaps carrying greatness of soul even to infirmity: it might be presumption for a man to put that trust in his fortunes, and to have that confidence in his own work in the world: but it is no undue confidence in us, and it savours of no presumption, to say to our anxious souls, when they distract us with fear for this life's provision and welfare, "Fear not: thou carriest a precious spirit bound for the blessed country afar: the Father of spirits breathed it into thee, the Son of God bled for it, the Holy Ghost guideth and sanctifieth it: thou art freighted with covenant promises, and the fruits of a Christian life stored up against the final harvest: be not thou troubled with daily wants and anxieties: only keep thine hand on the helm, and thine eye on the compass, and let the wild waves rage as they will. Seek first the one great purpose for which thou art, and all things else shall be added unto thee."

September 1865.

THE BOOK-LIST

OF

ALEXANDER STRAHAN.

𝔅ooks 𝔍ust 𝔓ublished.

HENRY HOLBEACH: STUDENT IN LIFE AND PHILOSOPHY.

A NARRATIVE AND A DISCUSSION.

With Letters to Mr Matthew Arnold, Mr Alexander Bain, Mr Thomas Carlyle, Mr Arthur Helps, Mr G. H. Lewes, Rev. H. L. Mansel, Rev. F. D. Maurice, Mr John Stuart Mill, and Rev. Dr J. H. Newman.

Two vols. post 8vo, 14s.

THE POETICAL WORKS OF HENRY ALFORD,

Dean of Canterbury.

A New and Enlarged Edition. Small 8vo.

IDYLS AND LEGENDS OF INVERBURN.

By ROBERT BUCHANAN,
Author of "Undertones."
Small 8vo, 5s.

UNDERTONES.

By ROBERT BUCHANAN.

Second Edition. Revised and Enlarged. Small 8vo, 5s.

ESSAYS ON WOMAN'S WORK.
By BESSIE RAYNER PARKES.
Small 8vo, 4s.

THE REGULAR SWISS ROUND, IN THREE TRIPS.
By the Rev. HARRY JONES,
Incumbent of St Luke's, Berwick Street, Soho, London.
With Illustrations. Small 8vo, 5s.

HEADS AND HANDS IN THE WORLD OF LABOUR.
By W. G. BLAIKIE, D.D., F.R.S.E.,
Author of "Better Days for Working People."
Crown 8vo, 3s. 6d.

THE COLLECTED WRITINGS OF EDWARD IRVING.
Edited by his Nephew, the Rev. G. CARLYLE, M.A.
Vols. I. to V., demy 8vo, 12s. each.

OUTLINES OF THEOLOGY.
By the late Rev. ALEXANDER VINET.
Post 8vo, 8s.

OUTLINES OF PHILOSOPHY AND LITERATURE.
By the late Rev. ALEXANDER VINET.
Post 8vo, 8s.

CHRIST AND HIS SALVATION.
By HORACE BUSHNELL, D.D.,
Author of "Nature and the Supernatural."
Second Edition. Crown 8vo, 6s.

CHRISTIAN COMPANIONSHIP FOR RETIRED HOURS.
Small 8vo, gilt, 3s. 6d.

LETTERS FROM ABROAD IN 1864.
By HENRY ALFORD, D.D.,
Dean of Canterbury.
Second Edition, Crown 8vo, 7s. 6d.

PLAIN WORDS ON CHRISTIAN LIVING.
By C. J. VAUGHAN, D.D., Vicar of Doncaster.
Small 8vo, 4s. 6d.

WOMAN'S WORK IN THE CHURCH:
BEING
HISTORICAL NOTES ON DEACONESSES AND SISTERHOODS.
By JOHN MALCOLM LUDLOW.
Small 8vo, 5s.

PERSONAL NAMES IN THE BIBLE.
By the Rev. W. F. WILKINSON, M.A.,
Vicar of St Werburgh's, Derby, and Joint-Editor of "Webster and Wilkinson's Greek Testament."
Small 8vo, 6s.

CONVERSION:
ILLUSTRATED FROM EXAMPLES RECORDED IN THE BIBLE.
By the Rev. ADOLPH SAPHIR.

New and Cheaper Edition. Small 8vo, 3s. 6d.

A YEAR AT THE SHORE.
By PHILIP HENRY GOSSE, F.R.S.
With Thirty-six Illustrations by the Author, printed in Colours by LEIGHTON BROTHERS.

Crown 8vo, 9s.

LAZARUS, AND OTHER POEMS.
By E. H. PLUMPTRE, M.A.,
Professor of Theology, King's College, London.

Second Edition. Small 8vo, 5s.

STUDIES FOR STORIES, FROM GIRLS' LIVES.
Cheap Edition. Crown 8vo, 6s.

DE PROFUNDIS: A TALE OF THE SOCIAL DEPOSITS.
By WILLIAM GILBERT,
Author of "Shirley Hall Asylum," &c.

2 vols. crown 8vo, 12s.

LILLIPUT LEVEE.
With Illustrations by J. E. MILLAIS and G. J. PINWELL.

Square 8vo, gilt, 5s.

DUCHESS AGNES, Etc.
By ISA CRAIG.
Second Edition. Small 8vo, cloth, 5s.

A PLEA FOR THE QUEEN'S ENGLISH.
By HENRY ALFORD, D.D.,
Dean of Canterbury.

Second Edition, Tenth Thousand. Small 8vo, 5s.

TANGLED TALK: An Essayist's Holiday.
Second Edition. Post 8vo, 7s. 6d.

OUR INHERITANCE IN THE GREAT PYRAMID.
By Professor C. PIAZZI SMYTH, F.R.SS.L. and E.,
Astronomer Royal for Scotland.

With Photograph and Plates. Square 8vo, 12s.

MEMOIRS OF THE LIFE AND PHILANTHROPIC LABOURS OF ANDREW REED, D.D.,
Prepared from Autobiographic Sources, by his Sons,
ANDREW REED, B.A., and CHARLES REED, F.S.A.
With Portrait and Woodcuts. Second Edition. Demy 8vo, 12s.

THE FOUNDATIONS OF OUR FAITH:
Ten Papers recently read before a Mixed Audience.
By Professors AUBERLEN, GESS, and Others.

Second Thousand. Crown 8vo, 6s.

STORY OF THE LIVES OF CAREY, MARSHMAN, AND WARD.

(A Popular Edition of the large Two-Volume Work.)

By JOHN C. MARSHMAN.

Sixth Thousand. Crown 8vo, 3s. 6d.

HUMAN SADNESS.

By the COUNTESS DE GASPARIN,
Author of "The Near and the Heavenly Horizons."

Fourth Thousand. Small 8vo, 5s.

The TWENTY-FOURTH THOUSAND is now ready of

THE RECREATIONS OF A COUNTRY PARSON.

First Series. Popular Edition.

Crown 8vo, 3s. 6d.

The THIRTY-SECOND THOUSAND is now ready of

THE GRAVER THOUGHTS OF A COUNTRY PARSON.

By the Author of "Recreations of a Country Parson."

Crown 8vo, 3s. 6d.

The FIFTEENTH THOUSAND is now ready of

COUNSEL AND COMFORT, SPOKEN FROM A CITY PULPIT.

By the Author of "Recreations of a Country Parson."

Crown 8vo, 3s. 6d.

The NINTH THOUSAND is now ready of
PAPERS FOR THOUGHTFUL GIRLS;
WITH SKETCHES OF SOME GIRLS' LIVES.
By SARAH TYTLER.
With Illustrations by MILLAIS. Crown 8vo, cloth extra gilt, 5s.

The THIRTY-EIGHTH THOUSAND is now ready of
SPEAKING TO THE HEART.
By THOMAS GUTHRIE, D.D.
Handsomely printed and bound in crown 8vo, 3s. 6d.
POCKET EDITION, small 8vo, 2s.

The SIXTH THOUSAND is now ready of
MY MINISTERIAL EXPERIENCES.
By the Rev. Dr BÜCHSEL, Berlin.
Crown 8vo, 3s. 6d.

The SECOND THOUSAND is now ready of
THE LIFE OF OUR LORD UPON THE EARTH,
CONSIDERED IN ITS HISTORICAL, GEOGRAPHICAL, AND GENEALOGICAL RELATIONS.
By the Rev. SAMUEL J. ANDREWS.
Crown 8vo, cloth, 6s. 6d.

The SIXTH THOUSAND is now ready of
DREAMTHORP;
A BOOK OF ESSAYS WRITTEN IN THE COUNTRY.
By ALEXANDER SMITH,
Author of "A Life Drama," &c.
Crown 8vo, 3s. 6d.

The SIXTEENTH THOUSAND is now ready of
THE EARNEST STUDENT:
BEING MEMORIALS OF JOHN MACKINTOSH.
By NORMAN MACLEOD, D.D.,
One of Her Majesty's Chaplains.
New Edition, considerably enlarged.
Crown 8vo, 3s. 6d.

The TENTH THOUSAND is now ready of
THE OLD LIEUTENANT AND HIS SON.
By NORMAN MACLEOD, D.D.
Crown 8vo, 3s. 6d.

The TENTH THOUSAND is now ready of
PARISH PAPERS.
By NORMAN MACLEOD, D.D.
Crown 8vo, 3s. 6d.

The TENTH THOUSAND is now ready of
THE GOLD THREAD: A STORY FOR THE YOUNG.
By NORMAN MACLEOD, D.D.
Illustrated by J. D. WATSON, GOURLAY STEEL, and J. MACWHIRTER.
Fine Edition, cloth gilt, 3s. 6d. Cheaper Edition, 2s. 6d.

The THIRTY-FIFTH THOUSAND is now ready of
WEE DAVIE.
By NORMAN MACLEOD, D.D.
Crown 8vo, 6d.

The THIRD THOUSAND is now ready of
WORDSWORTH'S POEMS FOR THE YOUNG.

Illustrated by MACWHIRTER and PETTIE, with a Vignette by MILLAIS.
Elegantly bound, in square crown 8vo, cloth gilt, 6s.

The SEVENTIETH THOUSAND is now ready of
BETTER DAYS FOR WORKING PEOPLE.
By WILLIAM G. BLAIKIE, D.D., F.R.S.E.

Crown 8vo, boards, 1s. 6d.

The FIFTEENTH THOUSAND is now ready of
PRAYING AND WORKING.
By Rev. W. FLEMING STEVENSON.

Crown 8vo, 3s. 6d.

The SIXTH THOUSAND is now ready of
FORTY YEARS' EXPERIENCE OF SUNDAY SCHOOLS.
By STEPHEN H. TYNG, D.D.

Foolscap 8vo, 1s. 6d.

The EIGHTH THOUSAND is now ready of
BEGINNING LIFE:
CHAPTERS FOR YOUNG MEN ON RELIGION, STUDY, AND BUSINESS.

By JOHN TULLOCH, D.D.,
Principal of St Mary's College, St Andrews.

Crown 8vo, 3s. 6d.

The SECOND THOUSAND is now ready of
GOD'S GLORY IN THE HEAVENS.
By WILLIAM LEITCH, D.D.,
Late Principal of Queen's College, Canada.
With Illustrations. Crown 8vo, cloth extra, 6s.

The TWENTY-FIFTH THOUSAND is now ready of
PLAIN WORDS ON HEALTH.
By JOHN BROWN, M.D.
Author of "Rab and his Friends," &c.
Small 8vo, 6d.

The TENTH THOUSAND is now ready of
THE THRONE OF GRACE.
By the Author of "The Pathway of Promise."
Foolscap 8vo, cloth antique, 2s. 6d.

The TWENTY-FOURTH THOUSAND is now ready of
ABLE TO SAVE;
Or, ENCOURAGEMENT TO PATIENT WAITING.
By the Author of "The Pathway of Promise."
Fcap. 8vo, cloth antique, 2s. 6d.

The NINETIETH THOUSAND is now ready of
THE PATHWAY OF PROMISE.
Neat cloth antique, 1s. 6d.

The TWENTY-SEVENTH THOUSAND is now ready of
THE NEAR AND THE HEAVENLY HORIZONS.
By the COUNTESS DE GASPARIN.
Crown 8vo, gilt cloth antique, 3s. 6d.

The FOURTH THOUSAND is now ready of
NATURE AND THE SUPERNATURAL,
AS TOGETHER CONSTITUTING THE ONE SYSTEM OF GOD.
By HORACE BUSHNELL, D.D.
Crown 8vo, 3s. 6d.

The SEVENTEENTH THOUSAND is now ready of
THE NEW LIFE.
By HORACE BUSHNELL, D.D.
Crown 8vo, 4s. 6d.; Cheap Edition, 1s. 6d.

The FIFTH THOUSAND is now ready of
CHRISTIAN NURTURE;
Or, THE GODLY UPBRINGING OF CHILDREN.
By HORACE BUSHNELL, D.D.
Crown 8vo, 1s. 6d.

The TWENTIETH THOUSAND is now ready of
THE CHARACTER OF JESUS.
By HORACE BUSHNELL, D.D.
Cheap Edition, 6d.

The FOURTH THOUSAND is now ready of
WORK AND PLAY.
A BOOK OF ESSAYS.
By HORACE BUSHNELL, D.D.
Crown 8vo, 3s. 6d.

The SECOND THOUSAND is now ready of
CHRISTIAN BELIEVING AND LIVING.
By F. D. HUNTINGDON, D.D.
Crown 8vo, cloth, 3s. 6d.

CHRISTINA, AND OTHER POEMS.
By DORA GREENWELL.
Small 8vo, 6s.

The THIRD EDITION is now ready of
THE PATIENCE OF HOPE.
By DORA GREENWELL.
Small 8vo, 2s. 6d.

The THIRD EDITION is now ready of
A PRESENT HEAVEN.
By DORA GREENWELL.
Small 8vo, 2s. 6d.

TWO FRIENDS.
By DORA GREENWELL.
Small 8vo, 3s. 6d.

The SIXTH THOUSAND is now ready of
THE WORDS OF THE ANGELS;
OR, THEIR VISITS TO THE EARTH AND THE MESSAGES THEY DELIVERED.
By RUDOLPH STIER, D.D.,
Author of "The Words of the Risen Saviour."
Crown 8vo, 2s. 6d.

The FOURTEENTH THOUSAND is now ready of
PERSONAL PIETY:
A HELP TO CHRISTIANS TO WALK WORTHY OF THEIR CALLING.
Cloth antique, 1s. 6d.

The TENTH THOUSAND is now ready of
AIDS TO PRAYER.
Cloth antique, 1s. 6d.

The TENTH THOUSAND is now ready of
THE SUNDAY-EVENING BOOK
OF PAPERS FOR FAMILY READING, BY

JAMES HAMILTON, D.D.	Rev. W. M. PUNSHON.
DEAN STANLEY.	JOHN EADIE, D.D., LL.D
Rev. THOMAS BINNEY.	J. R. MACDUFF, D.D.

Cloth antique, 1s. 6d.

The SIXTH THOUSAND is now ready of
THE POSTMAN'S BAG;
A STORY-BOOK FOR BOYS AND GIRLS.

By the Rev. J. DE LIEFDE, London,
Author of the "Pastor of Gegenburg."

With Sixteen full-page Illustrations. Square 8vo, cloth gilt, 3s. 6d.

THE RESTORATION OF THE JEWS:
THE HISTORY, PRINCIPLES, AND BEARINGS
OF THE QUESTION.

By DAVID BROWN, D.D.,
Professor of Theology, Aberdeen, Author of "The Second Advent."
Crown 8vo, 5s.

The TWENTY-SECOND THOUSAND is now ready of
THE HIGHER CHRISTIAN LIFE
By the Rev. W. E. BOARDMAN.
Foolscap 8vo, 1s. 6d.

The FORTIETH THOUSAND is now ready of
LIFE THOUGHTS.
By HENRY WARD BEECHER.
Cloth antique, 2s. 6d.

The SIXTH THOUSAND is now ready of
ROYAL TRUTHS.
By HENRY WARD BEECHER.
Crown 8vo, 3s. 6d.

The THIRD THOUSAND is now ready of
EYES AND EARS.
By HENRY WARD BEECHER.
Crown 8vo, 3s. 6d.

The THIRD THOUSAND is now ready of
ROMANISM AND RATIONALISM AS OPPOSED TO PURE CHRISTIANITY.
By JOHN CAIRNS, D.D.
Crown 8vo, 1s.

The TWENTIETH THOUSAND is now ready of
THE STILL HOUR.
By AUSTIN PHELPS.
Cheap Edition, 4d.

The THIRTY-SECOND THOUSAND is now ready of
BLIND BARTIMEUS AND HIS GREAT PHYSICIAN.
By the Rev. W. J. HOGE.
In neat cloth, 1s.

Forthcoming Books.

A SUMMER IN SKYE.
By ALEXANDER SMITH,
Author of "A Life Drama," "City Poems," &c.

Two vols. post 8vo, 16s. [*Ready.*

MILLAIS'S ILLUSTRATIONS:
BEING A COLLECTION OF HIS DRAWINGS ON WOOD.
By JOHN E. MILLAIS, R.A.

Royal 4to.

SIX MONTHS AMONG THE CHARITIES OF EUROPE.
By the Rev. JOHN DE LIEFDE, London.

With Illustrations. Two vols. post 8vo.

DAYS OF YORE.
By SARAH TYTLER,
Author of "Papers for Thoughtful Girls," &c.

Two vols. square 8vo.

JUDAS ISCARIOT:
A DRAMATIC POEM.

Small 8vo.

TRAVELS IN THE SLAVONIC PROVINCES OF TURKEY IN EUROPE.

Part I.

From the Ægean to the Adriatic, through Bulgaria and Old Serbia.

Part II.

From the Danube to the Adriatic, through Bosnia and the Herzegovina.

By G. MUIR MACKENZIE and A. P. IRBY.

With numerous Illustrations. Demy 8vo.

THE AUTOCRAT OF THE BREAKFAST-TABLE.

By OLIVER WENDELL HOLMES.

Small 8vo.

THE HYMNS AND HYMN WRITERS OF GERMANY.

By the Rev. W. FLEMING STEVENSON,

Author of "Praying and Working."

With New Translations of the Hymns by GEORGE MACDONALD, DORA GREENWELL, and L. C. SMITH.

Two vols. post 8vo.

FAMILY PRAYERS FOR THE CHRISTIAN YEAR.

By HENRY ALFORD, D.D., Dean of Canterbury.

Small 8vo.

www.ingramcontent.com/pod-product-compliance
Lightning Source LLC
Chambersburg PA
CBHW031350230426
43670CB00006B/493